TAOS INDIANS

TAOS INDIANS

Facsimile of Original 1925 Edition

by
Blanche Chloe Grant

New Foreword
by
Marcia Muth

SOUTHWEST HERITAGE SERIES

SUNSTONE PRESS

SANTA FE

Sunstone books may be purchased for educational, business, or sales promotional
use. For information please write: Special Markets Department, Sunstone Press,
P.O. Box 2321, Santa Fe, New Mexico 87504-2321.

Library of Congress Cataloging-in-Publication Data

Grant, Blanche C. (Blanche Chloe), 1874-1948.
  Taos Indians : facsimile of original 1925 edition / by Blanche Chloe Grant ; new fore-
word by Marcia Muth.
     p. cm. -- (Southwest heritage series)
  Includes bibliographical references and index.
  ISBN 978-0-86534-605-5 (softcover : alk. paper)
  1. Taos Indians--History. 2. Taos Indians--Social life and customs. 3. New Mexico--
History. I. Title.

E99.T2G8 2008
978.9004'97496--dc22

                              2007043005

WWW.SUNSTONEPRESS.COM
SUNSTONE PRESS / POST OFFICE BOX 2321 / SANTA FE, NM 87504-2321 /USA
(505) 988-4418 / ORDERS ONLY (800) 243-5644 / FAX (505) 988-1025

The Southwest Heritage Series is dedicated to Jody Ellis and Marcia Muth Miller, the founders of Sunstone Press, whose original purpose and vision continues to inspire and motivate our publications.

CONTENTS

I

THE SOUTHWEST HERITAGE SERIES

The history of the United States is written in hundreds of regional histories and literary works. Those letters, essays, memoirs, biographies and even collections of fiction are often first-hand accounts by people who wanted to memorialize an event, a person or simply record for posterity the concerns and issues of the times. Many of these accounts have been lost, destroyed or overlooked. Some are in private or public collections but deemed to be in too fragile condition to permit handling by contemporary readers and researchers.

However, now with the application of twenty-first century technology, nineteenth and twentieth century material can be reprinted and made accessible to the general public. These early writings are the DNA of our history and culture and are essential to understanding the present in terms of the past.

The Southwest Heritage Series is a form of literary preservation. Heritage by definition implies legacy and these early works are our legacy from those who have gone before us. To properly present and preserve that legacy, no changes in style or contents have been made. The material reprinted stands on its own as it first appeared. The point of view is that of the author and the era in which he or she lived. We would not expect photographs of people from the past to be re-imaged with modern clothes, hair styles and backgrounds. We should not, therefore, expect their ideas and personal philosophies to reflect our modern concepts.

Remember, reading their words and sharing their thoughts is a passport back into understanding how the past was shaped and how it influenced today's world.

Our hope is that new access to these older books will provide readers with a challenging and exciting experience.

II

FOREWORD TO THIS EDITION
by
Marcia Muth

Blanche Chloe Grant was born in 1874 in Leavenworth, Kansas. Like many other women of her time, she was from the first an independent spirit. She was interested in the arts and literature and saw a role for women that did not include the usually prescribed domestic life. A graduate of Vassar College, she also studied at the Boston Museum School of Fine Arts, The Pennsylvania Academy and the Art League in New York City. She soon became known for both her landscape paintings and her career as a magazine illustrator.

In 1918, she was asked to go to France as head of an art project under the auspices of the Y.M.C.A.

A move to Taos, New Mexico in 1920 brought about dramatic changes in Grant's life. She developed an intense interest in the rich and varied history of the area. She took on the job of editor of the *Taos Valley News* and began her years of research into the history of Taos and the Southwest. This led then to a series of books, many of which were about Taos and the people who lived there.

Her art also changed and she painted Native American and Western subjects. Although an active participant in the Taos art scene, she continued to show paintings in New York. Gradually her main interests turned to her writing. Her books included *When Old Trails Were New, Doña Lona* and she edited a biography of Kit Carson based on his notes.

After Grant got settled in Taos, she became interested in the Indians at Taos Pueblo. She became friends with tribal members, especially some of the elder members. They found her to be a sympathetic and trustworthy listener. She saw that inevitable changes were happening to the Native American culture and society. Their history which had been handed down generation to generation through oral means was now being fragmented and lost.

At the same time there was a national interest in the ways of Native Americans. This interest which was sparked by the end of the Mexican War in 1848 and the acquisition of new American territory had attracted a host of writers. While some were serious historians and anthropologists, there were others who stayed for a brief time, asking questions in a way that provoked unreliable answers from their sources. There was also the problem that some Native Americans felt it was wrong to share the facts about their history, customs and rites with outsiders.

The Taos Indians with their large population, colorful ceremonies and magnificent Pueblo structure were always of prime interest. They tried to balance between tradition and the new intrusions of the modern world. Grant understood the narrow line between the two worlds and respected it. She helped the Taos Indians that she knew understand the importance of having someone they trusted write down their words for posterity. It was not just for the Anglo world but for their own future generations.

In her own words, Grant gives the genesis of her purpose in writing this book. She said, "So much is slipping away that should be caught in hard print." Always seeing herself as historian, a conduit for facts, she reminds readers that this is not her story. She is only the recorder. That is why her tombstone bears this inscription: "Historian of Taos."

III

FACSIMILE OF 1925 EDITION

Taos Indians

B. C. Grant

INDIAN CAMP IN TAOS CAÑON.
Sept. 30, 1925.

Taos Indians

By
Blanche C. Grant

Taos, New Mexico
1925

SANTA FE NEW MEXICAN PUBLISHING CORPORATION

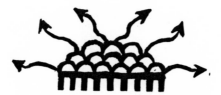

Indian design after a sketch drawn by Ad. F. Bandelier and designated by him as signifying thunderstorm and rain.

*To the Memory
of
Taos Braves who have gone to
the happy hunting ground
and
Indian women who, though un-
sung, have borne the greatest
burdens of life in the Taos
Pueblo.*

LIST OF ILLUSTRATIONS

Foreword.

Every now and then, some one, pencil in hand, comes to Taos, stays a few days, bent on questioning the Indians. Usually he puts his queries in the form of positive statements. To these the red man gives an easy affirmative. Then the stranger hurries away believing he knows all about the Indian. Not long ago, one of the older men was heard to give such answers. "What did you tell that fellow all those lies for, John," said a bystander later. "Oh," said the Indian with a faint smile, "He likes it."

Another Indian said quite frankly to me one day, "If you get it right, they will say it is not true." Still another Indian came to town and asserted positively, "Miss Grant has written a whole lot about us that isn't true at all." I had not yet written a single line of this study of the Taos Indian. So it is with some timidity that even a long-time resident speaks of our Indians.

There are some of the better educated Indians who believe it will be well if there be written down the truth about their people. The majority, however, are sure that their history sent down orally from generation to generation is all that is necessary to preserve the story of their forefathers for themselves. As for the rest of the world, why need they care? Of the change that comes to all people under the American flag they reck but little. They do not see the signs, though their wisest men are often forced to say, "We do not know." A young

Indian, when telling a story not long ago, ended by saying, "You see my grandfather tried to tell my father but he did not want to listen. So he told the story to me and I was only a little boy. I can not remember it all."

So much is slipping away that should be caught in hard print. Such has been my self-appointed task. Every possible care has been taken to cull the truth. Indian, Anglo and Spanish-Americans have all assisted me and for obvious reasons I am not at liberty to name them, but I believe their words worthy of credence.

Crowded into a pit are the scholars, the Indian has the stage. It is his legends, traditions and historic facts I have tried faithfully to present. These are so interwoven in the Indian's mind that, only with the greatest caution, can one pull from the tangle, the threads which weave themselves into a semblance of truth. Even at best, there may be faults in the weaving.

BLANCHE C. GRANT,

Taos, New Mexico,

April 30, 1925.

CAVE HOMES IN FRIJOLES CAÑON
Where Indians First Lived.

PUEBLO RUINS IN FRIJOLES CAÑON.
Indian Home after the day of the caves.

Taos Indians

PART I.
—1847

Far away to the north once lay a beautiful lake
and from its waters rose the Taos Indians. So runs
their story. They wandered south and at Abiqui met
other Indians who taught them how to live. They
built a pueblo at Ojo Caliente and long years passed.
Then they wandered even to the "Black Mountains,"
far, far south. Again mother followed mother. They
were happy—these children of the Sun. Then perhaps there was a great sickness. The time came to
move once more. They turned north, marching slowly for they had by this time large numbers of do-
mesticated turkeys which they drove before them.
Stopping on the way, they built a new pueblo and
lived for a generation or more.

Traveling north again these Indians came to a
good site for a home. Here part of the tribe decided
to stay and they became the Picuris. The others
came on into Taos valley and lived first over beyond
Llano on a lovely hill-top which, commanding a wide
view, gave them ample time to prepare when enemies
approached. There today are the ruins of home
walls. The circle of an early kiva has yet another
wall within it suggesting that the Indians returned
to rebuild the home their forefathers had left for
some unknown reason. Other pueblo walls, leveled

but not quite lost, suggest a journey which circled the
valley around to the west by Cordovas, then to the
Lobo on the north.   Perhaps it was there that their
boy chief, chosen at first in a spirit of fun, grew to
manhood and dominated the tribe so that when he
ordered once more a migration the Indians obeyed.
Some there were who would not follow then but later
made their way to the place of their present home
and became the Isleta tribe.   The main body of Indians, however, followed their great chief.   Above
them swung in the glinting sunlight an eagle which
led them south again and dropped two feathers near
a great rock-bound peak.   ''Here,'' spoke the eagle,
''You shall build two pueblos.''   Then he lifted his
great wings and was lost in the blue.[1]   So came the
Taos Indians into this valley, perhaps a thousand
years ago.   Perhaps two thousand years have swung
their way into the silence of the eternal past.   Who
knows?

The story of their life around the valley seems
fairly well based on facts if ruined walls and relics
speak truly.   Back of the last nine or ten hundred
years the scholar does not go, being unwilling to follow Indian tradition entirely. He learns a little about
a wonderful people to the south, the Mayas.   Did a
small group of these come a-wandering north and
thus escape the pestilence which seems to have swept
that southern land of all people?   Did they live on,
remembering for a time and then, forgetting, build
for themselves a new group of tales?

If not from the south, did the Indians come from

---

1. Chas. F. Lummis was probably the first to record this story.

the north which falls into the tradition of most of
the tribes now of the southwest? And wandering
from the north did they come long years ago when
tropical palms waved in the warm air of a land
now submerged with the icy waters of Behring
Straits? Or did tumbling junks from China's distant shore weigh anchor on the coast of lower California and, leaving their burden of souls seeking new
homes, set sail to bring more and never make the
land again? So reads Chinese history. Did they
find and mingle with ancient people or did sun
and wind beat them into a race quite unlike their
ancestors?

Close study of many an Indian child's face
makes that word *unlike* lose force. There is something strikingly Mongolian in the slanting eyes, high
cheek bones and round face of many a boy who,
grown to manhood, changes very markedly. The
child face remains a puzzle.

We are well aware of that argument of the prim-
itive ax. The one found on this continent is not like
that of old China. Could not the migrating Chinese
have stayed long enough on their wanderings afoot
to get a new idea for an ax? That ax does not cut
down the question to a bare No. What of the jade
found nowhere on this continent, yet discovered all
carved into quaint shapes among the ruined temples
of Old Mexico? Jade belonged to China before years
were counted.

Three years ago there came from far away Pek-
in a Chinese merchant into this Indian country. He
watched the Indian, wherever he met him. He used

some of the simpler Chinese words and the Taos
Indian understood! He found designs on Indian pottery—symbols, untold ages old in Asia. He found his
thoughts reverting. One evening he sat in my home
and, grasping at the arms of the rocker, leaned for-
ward and slowly in correct though bookish English,
finally gave expression to an opinion unusual to say
the least for a proud, educated Chinese. "I am sorry to say the Chinese scholars do not know much
about the Indian. The longer I am here and see the
Indian, the more I wonder if the Chinese did not
come from the Indian."

This the red man of today prefers to believe.
He is sure his was the first people. He does not
want to be linked up with the Chinese in any other
way. This came out one summer evening when a
group of Taos people sat in the patio of the Blumen-
schein studio home, a few years ago. J. J. Jeancon,
then of the Smithsonian, talked away the twilight
telling of his belief that the Indians had not been in
this country probably more than fifteen hundred
years and of the finding, not only of words in the
language but of bows, arrows and sculptured heads,
in the land north of Thibet or in Thibet itself that
correspond so much to Indian words and implements
as to be fairly identical. His story done, Mr. Jeancon
asked for questions. The white man had his say.
Last of all an Indian, Tony Romero, who had listened
carefully called out, "I want to ask one question,
Mr. Jeancon. How is it, if the Indians come from the
Chineeman, he change so quick?"

We know of one Indian who, spying a silver belt

MOONLIGHT LAKE SONG
Bert G. Phillips

buckle of Chinese character for design, walked up to the wearer and eagerly asked, "Where did you get that? It is like the writing on the rocks."

Yet another Indian went away into the woods with his artist master. Night came and both sat in a wooden shack. Beyond the partition two men were jabbering. The Indian listened attentively, turned and asked the painter, "Who's in the next room?"

"I do not know. Why, Manuel?"

"I hear sounds like my people but I can not make out the words."[1]

Behind the wall, busy with the preparation of the evening meal, were two Chinese cooks.

Now is the time to study that word "Taos" which has puzzled so many scholars. The word *Tao* is undoubtedly an Indian word though not commonly in use by our Indians. It seems to have been used by other tribes when referring to the red men of this valley. The Picuris far up in the mountains to the southwest are of the same tribe, descendants of those who weary of wandering refused to travel farther and settled down on that land which was to their liking. These called their brothers the *Tao*.[1] Oñate

2. It is well known that after Indians "came to live in a bunch," as one Taos put it, there were many tongues. Finally that of the "Pfia or feather clan" won out and is the language of the pueblo today. Clark Wissler—American Indians—1917.

Of this "Tewa speech" of the Taos who belong, according to scholars to Tanoan stock, J. P. Harrington writes, "Tewa speech is excessively nasal and much broken by the glottal stop. Like Chinese, it makes use of 'tones.' There are 45 distinct individual sounds—12 of these sounds are vowels and may be long or short." Bulletin No. 17, Arch. Inst. of America. Mr. Harrington also says, "The musical accent of the Taos language is identical with that of Chinese, and so are most of the sounds."

3. J. P. Harrington discovered this word "Tao" as Indian in origin in 1909.

In the Chaves edition of the play "Los Commanchos," written probably about 1781 by a soldier who passed through Taos with Juan Bautista de Anza in 1779, there appears this. One of the chiefs in boasting says, "I went as ambassador to the Tao."

heard the name and down in his journal was written for the first time the word *Táos* in 1598. Like other Spaniards he but added the "s" and made *Taos*.

Most of the Indians here admit that they do not know what the word means. Now and then, however, some of the older men have ventured to suggest a meaning. Several have said that it means, "A Gateway to Heaven" or an "Entry-way to Heaven,"—a charming name for the land at the mouth of the cañon which leads to their hunting ground as happy as any on this side of the great line of life. "Place of the Sacred Mountain" also comes from an Indian. Perhaps more interesting than all is the story of a wise man of the pueblo who said, recently, that, long, long ago, the Indians had a great chief Ta-oo and among their many gods was one "Aosi." He suggested a combination of the words might have produced *Taos*.

Tao—again the mind goes swiftly across the Pacific to ancient China. Ages ago there was a great philosopher Lao-tze who wrote a treatise called "Tao-Feh-King." That word *Tao* has for its usual meaning "The Way" or "The right way" and was in use long before the day of Lao-tze.

Are we not now on the right trail to the word "Taos", *Way—Heaven—Sacred*. Believers in *Tao* or the "right way", or followers of the great chief

---

3a. The Indians refer to their pueblo as "Te-ha-ta" but this is a word common among Indians for home or place of the folk. It can not be considered a specific name. They speak of themselves as "Red Willow Indians" and when one sees their stream he understands why. Not long ago an Indian gave the following name for their home—"E-ah-sla-fai-mo Ba-he-a-thel-ba," which means Willows-red-cañon." The Apaches, I believe, have a name for these Indians unlike the word Taos and it means "Red Willow Indians."

Ta-oo might easily have been called the *"Tao* In-dians."

The Taos Indians, ages ago, undoubtedly made human sacrifices to their gods as did the Chinese. There is among the great rocks east of Arroyo Seco a great cave with a high flat rock, slightly larger than a human figure. This of itself would mean nothing but the Indians know of it as an ancient ceremonial cave. Some years ago an artist and his model camped near this place. Night came. A cheery camp fire blazed but the Indian's eyes wandered from it again and again into the darkness. Leaves lifted and rustled. Gusts of wind carried unsteady light against the rock shapes. The artist after a while slept but not so the Indian. Midnight came and passed. At about one, the Indian touched his sleeping comrade and in awed voice said, "Let us go." Reassured by his white friend, the red man was quiet once more. In the early morning he declared emphatically that he would not stay there another night adding, "There are too many brujos (spirits) around here."

Caves, words, symbols,[4] religious rites and certain characteristics of dress and children's faces seem to bear out the belief that somewhere, sometime there was relationship between the Indians and the Chinese. In the middle of the nineteenth century

---

4. Some years ago a prominent Taos physician and another stumbled upon a shrine of the Picuris Indian used in their phallic ceremonies. The symbol found is one so common all over China and gives all honor to man, as far as race propagation is concerned.

4a. J. G. Bourke in his study called "Superstitions of the Rio Grande" refers to the use of the black cat's flesh and blood as a cure for consumption. He adds, "The analogy of this notion can be traced in the far East. It is believed by Chinamen that cat's meat is a remedy for lung trouble diseases."

many held to the theory[5] that these were the descendants of the ''lost tribes'' of Jews but the scholar today discards this and swings toward the belief that
these people once belonged to each other in the past
which is so far away that none may ever truly know.

Whether the belief of a link between the Indian
and the Chinese is tenable or not, it is certainly true
that the Taos Indians of today are the result of a
mingling of many races of Indians. There is a per-
sistent tradition that some two or more centuries
ago the Apache and Utes swept through the country
and, conquering, killed all the men and boys and
took over the Taos pueblo. There are too many types
of Indian, according to facial characteristics alone,
at the final home of all the Indians of the valley
where they gathered for safety, not to believe that
they number among their ancestors many tribes of
the southwest.

Taos Indians have earned through the centuries
the name of being peaceful, home-loving people.
They were never been given to fighting for the love
of it, though they knew how when pressed to the
wall by roving Commanches who after traveling for
many moons came into this country about 1714.
They, with the Apaches and Utes, often made war
on this pueblo.

As to their communal houses, there are several
tales. One who claims to have heard the story, over
and over again, from the old men of his family told
me that the first pueblos, two of them, were just

5. Rev. Samuel Parker wrote at length on this subject when he
traveled across the continent in 1835.

PUEBLO RUINS NEAR LLANO, TAOS VALLEY.

KIVA RUINS NEAR LLANO, TAOS VALLEY

east of the present buildings and that they were
first fired by Indians. Indians fought Indians. The
Taos fled to the hills. Then rose the flames of burning homes but they did not entirely destroy the whole
pueblo which was repaired and used for some time.
Then came the Spaniards and the Indians say they
were the ones who finally razed the two pueblos to
the ground. Spaniards with De Vargas admitted
sacking the pueblo before they turned south but said
nothing about setting the place on fire. That there
was a great conflagration is an established fact,
however, and it probably took place in the late sixteen hundreds. Home builders of this generation
tell of finding burnt corn and ashes on the site of
some of the more easterly homes of the present
group of buildings.

Some years passed, perhaps a few, perhaps
thirty, as one Indian put it because at that time, he
said, they elected head men every ten years and
three men or groups of men had been in office. The
Indians contented themselves with small shelters in
their cañon. There are ruins of adobe homes even
now up the sides of the cañon which have been
thought by some to have been homes of Spaniards
but Indians claim they never lived in their Glorieta
cañon.

When the first Spaniards came across the plains
in 1541 there seems to have been one more venture-
some than the others. He came riding ahead on his
burro. The Indians had never seen such an animal
nor such a man. They believed this was a sort of
elk bringing into their midst a god or spirit. Then

followed others of these strangers with their bright
dress, glittering spears and breastplates. The Indians came out to meet them. Neither could understand the other. Sign language helped Coronado's
Captain Alvarado in 1540 and Barrioneuvo some
months later. They "left the province in peace"
runs the record. Then for long years the old men
told tales to their children of a strange people who
came and went away and never returned.

The days of 1598 brought another group of these
people over the trail from Picuris. Oñate brought
with him priests. Again the Indians greeted the
strangers in a friendly manner. They watched the
long-robed friars move among the soldiers quietly
and say strange words when they lifted a small
crossed stick. They too had a cross symbol sacred
to them. They watched with wonder while the fathers held out their hands in blessing. They began to
understand that such men "made good medicine."
Then came the new name. These were "Blessing
people" or "Quah-nah'"[6] a name still used when referring to Mexicans. They submitted to baptism for
that they thought was part of the "good medicine."

When the first church was to be built, the friars
had the Indians drag or carry on their shoulders
great rocks for the foundation of the building. Lazy
Indians felt the whip of their friar master. This
they did not forget. There were some things that did

----

6. Here I have used the meaning given by an old Indian. I have
been told, however, that students of the Taos language translate
this word, "Armoured people." It may have been possible that
there were two names similar in sound. It is evident that the
Indians remember the friars as men who blessed their people.

not seem to come as a true result of that good medicine he was supposed to have brought.

It may be well now to unfold papers which lie yellowing among the archives in Seville, Spain. One of the keepers of these valuable old documents—an American woman, Irene Wright of Colorado,—said not long ago that some of the papers still have on them the sand thrown there almost four hundred years ago by the writers who scratched away in their journals when they came through our valley. Fortunately there have been a few who have been eager for news of those years and we are the richer by translations. I have culled the few paragraphs which refer directly to the Pueblo of Taos—the very first written words one may find.

Castañeda wrote about 1561 his recollections of the expedition of Coronado of which he had been a member. Coronado's own journal never has been found. As far as we know he himself never came to Taos valley. Indians have said that they have, among their archives, a journal of one of these early leaders who, on leaving the pueblo intrusted his precious records to the Indians who swore to keep them until he should return. He never came back but they still keep their faith. Never do they unlock for the stranger their strong box which passes to each governor in turn. If the box holds real secrets, it holds them well.

"There was a large and powerful river," wrote Castañeda, "I mean village, which was called Braba, 20 leagues farther up the river, which our men called

Valladolid.[7] The river flowed through the middle
of it. The natives crossed it by wooden bridges,
made of very long, large squared pines.[8] At this village they saw the largest and finest hot rooms or
estufas that there were in the entire country for they
had a dozen pillars, each one of which was twice as
large around as one could reach and twice as tall as
a man. Hernando de Alvarado visited this village
when he discovered Cicuye. The country is very
high and very cold. The river is deep and very swift
without any ford. Captain Barrionuevo returned
from here, leaving the province at peace." July,
1542.[9]

Captain Juan Jaramilla, another who was with
Coronado, wrote as follows:

"At the river of Tihuex there are 15 villages
within a short distance of about 20 leagues, all with
flat-roof houses or earth, instead of stone, after the
fashion of mud walls. There are other villages besides these on other streams which flow into this,
and three of these are, for Indians, well worth seeing, especially one that is called Chia (Zia) and
another Uraba (Taos) and another Cicuique (Pe-
cos). Braba and Cicuique have many houses two
stories high. All the rest, and these also, have corn
and beans and melons, skins and some long robes of
the feathers which they braid joining the feathers
with a sort of thread and they also make them of a
sort of plain weaving with which they make the
cloaks with which they protect themselves. They all

7. The town, valley and river in Spain are similar to that of the
pueblo and its surroundings in our country.
8. The river is still so crossed.
9. Translation by G. P. Winship.

have hot rooms underground, which, although not very clean, are very warm. They raise and have a very little cotton of which they make the cloaks which I have spoken of above.''[10]

Still another whose name is lost wrote of Taos. He too was evidently with Coronado. ''This river rises where these settlements end at the north, on the slope of the mountains there, where there is a large village different from the others, called Yuraba (Taos). It is settled in this fashion. It has 18 divisions, each one has a situation as if for two ground plots; the houses are very close together and have five or six stories, three of them with mud walls and two or three with thin wooden walls, which become smaller as they go up and each one has its little balcony outside of the mud walls, one above the other, all around of wood. In this village as it is in the mountains they do not raise cotton nor breed fowls (turkeys); they wear skins of the deer and cows (buffalos) entirely. It is the most populous village of all that country. We estimated there were 15000 souls in it.''[11]

Of the life of that day we again turn to Castañeda who, writing about the Indians of Tiguex and the neighborhood which meant the pueblos of the upper Rio Grande including Taos probably, noted down these facts which tally well with manners of today.

''They keep the separate houses where they prepare the food for eating and where they grind the

10. Translated by Chas. Parker Winship. 14th Annual Report of Bureau of Ethnology, 1896.
11. Translated by A. F. Bandelier. In Seville this is recorded under date of 1531 but undoubtedly refers to 1540-1. The number of 15000 is considered a gross exaggeration.

meal, very clean. This is a separate room or closet,
where they have a trough with three stones fixed in
stiff clay. Three women go in here, each one having
a stone, with which one of them breaks the corn, the
next grinds it and the third grinds it again. They
take off their shoes, do up their hair, shake their
clothes and cover their heads before they enter the
door. A man sits at the door playing on a fife while
they grind, moving the stones to the music and singing together. They grind a large quantity at one
time, because they make all their bread soaked in
warm water, like wafers. They gather a great
quantity of brushwood and dry it to use for cooking
all through the year. There are no fruits good to
eat in the country except the pine nuts.''

Further Castañeda wrote of Indians in general
what was probably true of our Indians as well.
''They go like Arabs with their tents and their
droves of dogs[12] harnessed with saddle cloths and
pack saddles and a cinch. When their load shifts,
the dogs howl for some one to straighten it out for
them.''

Of this custom still another wrote, in 1599.

''To carry this load, the poles that they use to
set it up, (referring to their well-tanned hide tents)
and a knapsack of meat and their *pinole*, or maize,
the Indians use a medium-sized dog, which is their
substitute for mules. They drive great trains of
them. Each girt around its breast and haunches,
and, carrying a load of flour of at least one hundred
pounds, travels as fast as his master. It is a sight

12. Dogs are no longer so used.

worth seeing and very laughable to see them traveling, the ends of the poles dragging on the ground,
nearly all of them snarling in their encounters,
traveling one after another on their journey. In
order to load them the Indian women seize their
heads between their knees and thus load them, or
adjust the load, which is seldom required, because
they travel along at a steady gait as if they had been
trained by means of reins.'"[13]

By 1630, appeared a similar statement by Benavides who said, ''When the Indians go off to trade
the whole rancherias go, with their women and children. They live in tents made of buffalo's hide, very
thin and tanned, and these tents they carry on pack
trains of dogs, harnessed with their pack saddles.
The dogs are medium sized and it is customary to
have 500 dogs in one pack train one in front of another and thus the people carry their merchandise
laden, which they barter for cotton cloth and other
things they need.'"[14]

Apparently some Spaniards came up into the
valley and settled soon after 1600 and lived either
right in the pueblo or very near it. So goes the Indian's story. By 1630 there was reported to the
Spanish King a flourishing church of 2500 baptised
souls. The monk, just quoted, Benavides, was sent
on a trip of investigation through New Mexico. He
came to Taos in 1627 and wrote of the conditions of
affairs as satisfactory. His account of our Indians
runs:

13.   1599.   Relaciones que envio Don Juan de Oñate de algunas jorna-
         das.   Translated by Herbert Eugene Bolton.
14.   Translation used in "The Great Plains" by Randall Parrish.

"These Indians are very well instructed, and last year 1627 the Lord confirmed his holy word by a miracle among them; and it was as follows; it was hard for them to give up having many wives, as they used to have before being baptized and the Religious daily preached to them the truth of the Holy Sacrament of Matrimony and the one who most gainsayed was an old Indian sorceress, who under pretext of going to the field for wood took four other women, good Christians, married according to the rules of our holy mother of the Church and going and returning she kept persuading them not to consent to the mode of marriage which the Father taught, that what they used in their paganism was better. The poor Christians kept resisting this and being now near the pueblo and the sorceress still keeping on her discourse the sky being clear and serene, a thunderbolt fell and killed that infernal ministress of the devil in the midst of the good Christian women, who resisted her evil doctrine and who remained entirely unhurt by the thunderbolt, and strongly confirmed in the truth of the holy Sacrament of Matrimony. The whole pueblo at once hastened there and seeing that blow of heaven all who were secretly in concubinage got married and believed sincerely all that the Father taught them, who at once made them a sermon on the event and he preaches to them every holiday as is done in other convents."[15]

It seemed well to the wandering friar to report

15. Memorial on New Mexico, 1826, by Alonso de Benavides, Custos of the Conversions of New Mexico. Mss. in New York Public Library. Addressed to King Philip IV. Printed in Spanish, Madrid, 1630. Translated by John G. Shea.

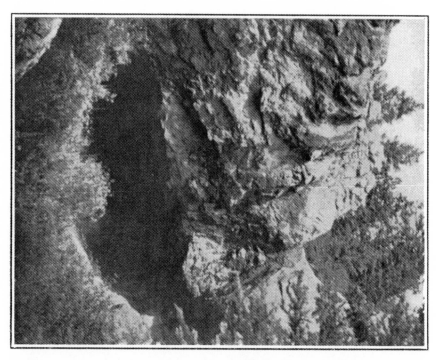

THE CEREMONIAL CAVE, NEAR ARROYO SECO.

THE DITCH OF 1818, NEAR ARROYO SECO.

nothing ill of all the Missions of course even if he
stretched the truth till it cracked his whole story. All
was not well, however. The lashes on tired backs
still cut deep into the Indian soul. These new people
were so near they were troublesome probably. Perhaps they reckoned if the friar was killed they would
all go away. At any rate, one cold December night,
the Spanish soldier sentinels went inside to get warm
believing the friar and themselves safe. Once within they soon found they were trapped and they did
not live to tell their story. This happened in 1631.
Whether there were other Spaniards near, the records do not say but the Indians say they were here
and apparently did not run away and later another
priest came to take up the work of Padre Miranda.[16]

By 1650, it seems another church was to be built.
The people had not forgotten the experience their
fathers had had with those heavy rocks nor the lash-
ing for lagging behind. It was about then that the
Taos Indian men met in their estufas in most solemn
conclave. The question was whether they should not
try to get rid of the Spaniards, priest and all. Deer
skins[17] were procured and the village scribe wrote
the picture message which all Indians would understand asking them to join in a revolt. Fleet runners
started with this call to war against the whites. It
went as far as the Moquis. These refused to join
and so nothing came of the mutterings in the Taos
kivas. Dissatisfied with this, perhaps wanting other
trading grounds, perhaps because they did not want

16. Miranda is the name believed to be that of this particular priest.
His name is still given to a cañon west of town.
17. Otermin Extractos—Bolton Collection, Berkeley, California.

to drag any more heavy stones,—the reason the Indians themselves give—a group of families left for
the east, never to return though Spanish records say
a messenger was sent after these wanderers some
seventy years later and that they returned. Not all
returned if any did. There are in Oklahoma, I am
told, a small group of Indians who claim to be the
descendants of these Taos Indians. Another party
of Indians probably later went west according to the
Indians. These two groups of people the Taos have
lost but not forgotten. Often a traveling Indian of
this tribe talks away the hours with some newly-
made Indian friends to see if, by any chance, they
belong to his people who went away and never came
back.

        *   *   *   *   *   *

The late seventies of the seventeenth century
were days when the Taos Indians were made most
uneasy. They heard of the killing and whipping of
some of their San Ildefonso friends to the south.
These "Blessing People" were far from being de-
sirable. They were a great disappointment. Taos
pueblo was far enough north so that it was not easily
reached by Spanish soldiers. They were a strongly
fortified people and may have considered themselves
as they do today as the most powerful and aristo-
cratic of all the Pueblo Indians. It is not surpris-
ing then, that Popé, the Tesuque Indian, who had
wandered far, learned many tricks and became a sort
of wonder to all the tribes decided that the Taos pue-

blo was the place for him to come and plot. The Taos
Indians received him cordially and listened atten-
tively. There still was much muttering against the
Spanish intruders.

Finally, one dark night, below in a still darker
kiva Popé played his final trump card. He caused
three Indians covered with phosphorus, probably,
to appear as spirits and support him in his plans.
Then the Indians were sure he was their leader.
Again a cord of yucca knotted to tell of days yet
to come went out from the pueblo by the swiftest
runners. This time even the far away Moquis were
willing. No Indian woman was allowed to tell the
secret but, of course, the men told themselves.

Some were forced to do so after an arrest at
Santa Fé; others were probably friendly with their
Spanish masters and it was no wonder that the dire
plans were discovered. But Popé was too good a
leader to lose. Another message of yucca went the
rounds and three days early the fury broke. Taos
Indians and others killed all they could about the
pueblo and swept southward to surround Santa Fé.
The story of the fleeing Spaniards need not be repeated here. Suffice it to say they surely fled.

The next year the Governor Otermin returned
and during the course of much inquiry the following
testimony was taken.

"It happened," runs the record of Indians tes-
tifying in 1681, "that in an estufa of the pueblo of
Taos there appeared to the said Indian Popé three
figures of Indians who never came forth from the
estufa. They gave him to understand that they went

under ground to the lagune of Copiala. These three
forms he saw emit fire from all the extremities of
their bodies, one of them was called Caudi, the other
Tilim and the third Heume. They spoke to the said
Popé and told him to make a string of yucca, tying in
it a number of knots in token of the days they had to
wait until they should break out and to send the said
string through all the villages of the kingdom, and
that the man who carried it should untie one knot
for each day in token of compliance and that by the
number of remaining knots they should know the
days yet lacking; this was commanded under penalty
of death. As soon as the treason was accomplished
they were to raise a smoke in each village of the
pueblos. The string was carried from village to village by the swiftest runners.''[18]

"After the uprising, continues the Indian tale
in the archives, ''Popé proclaimed in the pueblos that
the devil was much stronger than God and better
than God, telling them to burn their images, temples,
rosaries and crosses, that the people might forsake
the wives married in holy matrimony, they should
not mention God and that they would receive the lash
if they did so and ordered that the Spanish language
should not be spoken and the seeds of the Spaniards
should be burned.'' Then Juan de Tesuque conclud-
ed by saying, ''All of the nations obeyed everything
except the command relative to the seeds of the Spaniards as some planted because they had the Spaniards in their hearts.''

*   *   *   *   *   *

18. Twitchell's "Leading Facts in New Mexican History."

Following the taking of much testimony from Indians, Otermin did attempt to reconquer the land in a half-hearted manner. Here and there he captured a stray Indian who was given trial whether there was a definite charge against him or not. Among these fellows was a Taos Indian a little more daring than some of the others. The complete record of this first known trial, never before presented. will surely be of interest.

RECORDS OF THE TRIAL OF AN APOSTATE
TAOS INDIAN AT CAMP OF SAN LORENZO
LATESMA...............AUGUST 11, 1682.

The Decree[19]

At the camp of San Lorenza Latesma(?) 11th August, 1682, the Army Master Francisco Xavier, Alcalde, Judge of Administration appointed with full power to receive and hear cases by Sr. Don Antonio de Otermin, Governor and Captain General of New Mexico authorized by H. M. reports that in the matter of what has been committed by an Indian, native of the Pueblo of Taos, of the rebel apostates of New Mexico, he left this camp on his return towards the regions of New Mexico in search of the now rebel apostates, and to proceed against him according to the official order of Royal Justice, I name in this decree as accompanying witnesses Sergeant Major Luis de Quintana and Antonio de Azala to assist me in the steps that must be taken in the oper-

19. Archive in Santa Fe Museum.

ation of this commission. I sign this with the witnesses.

> Francisco Xavier (Rubric)
> Luis de Quintana (Rubric)
> Antonio de Azala (Rubric)

First Testimony

At the camp of San Lorenzo de Latesma(?) on the Rio del Norte' August 13, 1682, I, the Judge of the commission for this case caused the accompanying witnesses to appear before me and also Sergeant Major D. Lopez Sambrano, witness in this aforesaid case for the security of this realm, from whom I took oath in due form by God Our Lord and a sign of the Cross, by which he swore to tell the truth as to what he knew, upon being questioned. Having been asked if he knew whether this Indian was one of the idolatrous rebels of New Mexico, he said he knows him very well and that several days ago, because of having received notice that he had fled after being captured, he went out with his squadron and crossed the Rio del Norte and, finding traces of him, followed him in the direction of New Mexico and overtook him, finding him hidden in a thicket, having on his person a ring and leg irons on his legs and he captured him and held him prisoner (words illegible) and he, personally, knew that the said Indian appeared to have been in company of two of the worst having been talking with them where he captured him, two (words illegible) who were mounted and to make very sure he sent Captain Francisco de Anaza with five other men to follow the other two

(two words illegible) on horseback, but they having
gone ahead from the place where the said Juan Cucala was and they had escaped, so the said Captain
Francisco de Anaza told him.

Asked what he thinks or what his opinion is of
the said Indian Cucala, he says that he knows the
action of said Indian and the opinion he has of him
is that the said Indian is a traitor, apostate to the
faith and one of those who rebelled in New Mexico
and that afterward, at the seige the Lord Captain
General put to the Pueblo of Isleta, in which this
witness took part, the said Indian was among the
others who were captured there and after being
freed and pardoned, he fled after two days and they
found him hidden in a wood on the bank of the Rio
del Norte; that from said pueblo where he was captured until today when he attempted to return to
his idolatry he went from crime to crime. He affirms that what he has said is the truth, and what
he, the witness, knows and according to his oath,
which he reaffirms upon reading of the above, his
testimony, and says it is the truth. He is 43 years
old, more or less and has sworn truthfully, as he
affirms, and signs with me and the witnesses.

> Diego Lopez (Rubric)
> Francisco Xavier (Rubric)
> Luis de Quintana (Rubric)
> Antonio de Azala (Rubric)

Second Testimony

At the camp of San Lorenzo de Latesma, Aug.
14, 1682, in the prosecution of this case and the cita-
tion made of Sergeant Major D. Lopez Zambrano of

Captain Francisco de Anaza, I had the latter appear before me and received from him an oath in due form by God Our Lord and a Sign of the Cross, upon charge whereof he swore to tell the truth, and having admitted the subpoena he said that what was said in regard to him by Sergeant Major Diego Lopez is the truth and he (D. L. Zambrano) saw that this witness was one of those present when they captured the said Juan Cucala, who was fleeing toward New Mexico and they found him hidden among some thickets, caught by his leg-irons and this witness went on to (word illegible) with two troopers. He saw them (the rest of the party) returning to this camp. He knows that he (Cucala) is one of the rebel idolaters of New Mexico and the witness saw that in the siege the Lord General laid to the pueblo of Isleta—he having been in it—one of the notable captives taken was the said Cucala among others and he was absolved and set free. He saw him that day at the said pueblo and two days later they found him hidden in some woods and saw him caught and he was made prisoner and brought to this camp, whence, after about a year had passed he saw how said (prisoner) attempted to return to idolatry and what he has said is the truth, and what he knows. This he affirms when it has been read to him and signs it. He is 48 years old, more or less, and he signed with me and the witnesses present.

Francisco de Anaza (Rubric)

Francisco Xavier (Rubric)

Antonio de Azala (Rubric)

Luis de Quintana (Rubric)

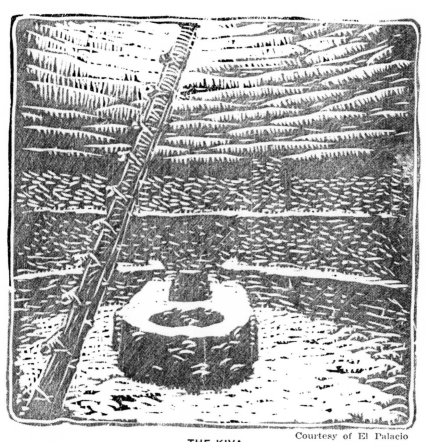

THE KIVA
Gustav Baumann

Third Testimony—The Prisoner.

In the Camp of San Lorenzo de Latesma, August 15, 1682, the prosecution of the case orders to appear before me Juan Cucala and the assisting witnesses to take his confession, Cecilio de la Cruz serving as interpreter. The oath being given to him, I caused to appear before me the said Juan Cucala, from whom I took oath in due form by God Our Lord and a sign of the Cross upon which he promised to speak the truth. Having been asked his name and of what place he is a native and his age, he says his name is Juan Cucala, that he is a native of the pueblo of Taos, that he does not know his age and has no profession, and that is the truth.

Asked why he took a ring of the irons off his leg, attempting to escape from the prisoners and was going toward New Mexico, he says so as not to meet his end, and that is the truth.

Asked why he was trying to return to apostacy among the rebels and though in fear of the land of hostile Indians where he might be killed, he said because his wits had deserted him and because (words illegible) to return among the apostates, and this is the truth.

Asked why, having been lost and then absolved of the crimes he had committed in having been a traitor, rebelling, denying the law of God, returning to the ancient idolatry of his ancestors and taking part in the murders, rapes and other atrocities they committed, he said that the cause which moved him is that he has not a good heart, knowing the purport of the question, and pressed in the matter he said he

did not wish to reply. He added persistently that all
he had done was because of a bad heart and that he
has no more to say. He maintains that what he has
said is the truth and affirms it. He did not sign, as
he did not know how to read or write. I signed this
with the witnesses.

>   Francisco Xavier (Rubric)
>   Luis de Quintana (Rubric)
>   Antonio de Azala (Rubric)

The Sentence

August 17, 1682, I, the said Alcalde and Judge
Registrar, having seen these papers and declara-
tions of witnesses and the confession of Juan Cucala,
Indian, one of the apostate rebels of New Mexico,
and, after having been pardoned and absolved, per-
sistent in his evil, adding crime upon crime, and he
fled from this camp being shackled with leg-irons—
which he had removed from one leg—and after his
escape he was captured by a guard of soldiers in
charge of Sergeant Major D. Lopez Sambrano, first
witness in these papers and moreover beside the said
crimes in which the said Indian was involved, he has
been a traitor, renegade, apostate and united and
joined, with those other two, in treacherous murders, atrocious robbery of churches and burnings of
sacred things and images. There is no safety for him
(means of keeping him safely) in this camp, as he
knows the Apache tongue and that of the Juinse.
Ruin might easily occur, wherefor, and because of
the crimes he has committed, and the flight in which
he was captured, having (viewed it) with all pity for

him and (consideration) for his paucity of understanding and his barbarism.

In view of this

With careful attention to the merits of the case
and the blame that results against the defendant, I
see fit to condemn, the said Indian, Juan Cucala to
be taken from this place and imprisoned in the town
of Corral or Señora where he shall be sold (words
illegible) for a period of four years, to run from the
hour when he shall be purchased by virtue of this
sentence and furthermore as to the (word illegible)
which shall be sufficient assurance, and the (word
illegible) in such quantity given for him and the ex-
penses of justice, costs of the case now closed (words
illegible) as Señor Don Antonio de Otermin, Govern-
or and Captain General of the Realm and House of
New Mexico and its environs for H. M. shall direct,
to whom I now render the papers and these documents shall be furnished to His Lordship (that he
may determine) the propriety thereof, and may he be
pleased to give his verdict on the sentence therein
that it may be handed over to the prisoner so that
he may be taken to be sold, judging of my announce-
ment and order, and I signed this as judge Percep-
tor with the witnesses, ordering that the said Juan
Cucala be notified of it.

Francisco Xavier (Rubric)

Luis de Quintana (Rubric)

Antonio de Azala (Rubric)

The camp, on the aforesaid day, month and year,
I the said Judge of Commission, the assisting witnesses being present, notified Juan Cucala Indian of

the sentence, who said that he had heard it and will fulfill it. He did not sign, not knowing how. I signed it, with the witnesses.

Francisco Xavier (Rubric)

Luis de Quintana (Rubric)

Antonio de Azala (Rubric)

So runs the record of Juan Cucala as translated by Fayette S. Curtis Jr., whose comment on the case is well worth quoting. He says, "The exact circumstances on which the trial was based are none too clear but apparently poor John got caught at Isleta, was pardoned and absolved, stayed with the Spaniards a year, and then decided to skip, but got caught at it. He would seem to have been rather a hard case, anyway, but his frank avowal that he had a "bad heart", i. e. just naturally felt like raising hell, is rather refreshing. Apparently, the judges felt so, too, as the sentence was certainly rather light."[20]

*   *   *   *   *   *

When in 1692, Don Diego de Vargas came marching northward, determined to conquer all the Indians, he had hard work with the Taos and made more than one trip into the valley. In 1696, he made his last and successful demand that the Taos surrender. He kept a journal which has only in very recent years been translated. As to his experience here, at that time, even though it may be somewhat lengthy, we believe in letting him tell his own story.

---

20. Letter from Fayette Curtis, Jr., to the author, Jan. 22, 1925.

WHAT DON DIEGO DE VARGAS WROTE ABOUT HIS VISIT TO TAOS, IN 1696.

(Translation in Twitchell's Leading Facts in New Mexican

History. Vol. II, Page 405.)

"On the twenty-second day of the month of Sept., of this date and year, (1696) I, said Govr. & Capt. Genl., having arrived with the said Army at Miranda, and having changed horses there because the Village of Taos is four leagues further, I left the said Army, with order to said Ensign Joseph Dominquez to go on to the said Village, while I did so with a detachment of twenty men, my lieutenant and the army commanders and officers, (in order) to see if there were any of the rebels in the said village or scattered in the fields, and, having entered it, nobody was found there and some Indian men and women were seen to be in the fields who betook themselves to flight, and, following them up to the Mesa, in front of their Pass, they began to send up their warning fires to their said People, some of whom, coming out of the entrance, I called upon them, through interpreters, and my lieutenant, to deliver the Blessed Virgin, the Church Ornaments, and the two captives they held; that they might be sure (that) I would pardon them and they could come down to their village, and I would return without doing any harm to their fields; and, for answer, they repeated their fires, and although on my side I had the said requisition made to them repeatedly, with the kindest words, in order to reassure them and quiet any suspicions they might entertain; it was in

keeping with their crime and the answer they gave
(was) that some arrows were discharged at some of
our friendly Indians, provoking a fight, as they replied with some shots, and in order to make disposi-
tion of the army, which had reached the said village,
as it was already late, I retired, and on the road a
soldier informed me that he had captured the Coyote
woman, Geromilla, which was a great satisfaction
(to me) because of getting information she had about
the said rebels for effective use in the battle pending
for the next day; and so I quartered the army in the
lodgings of the said Taos, which were the only ones
(and were) surrounded by a wall; and in witness
whereof, I signed with my Civil and Mil'y Sec'y.

Sept. 23, 1696.

"On the twenty-third day of the month of Sept.,
of this date and year, I, said Govr. and Capt. Genl.,
having given orders to the Chiefs and Officers of the
Army to select a detachment of the cavalry Guard,
which under its commander should retire into the
country, but in sight of the said village, and to mount
the remainder of the men, and provide them with ammunition, and at the same time, the War-captains,
with their Indians, should go out, and the said order
having been carried out in this manner, the said soldiers being mounted as a Squadron, I said Govr. &
Capt. Genl., also mounted, and with the Rev. Father
Preacher Fray Blas Navarro, who was Chaplain of
the said Army, and with the said troop of horse, took
the road going into the Pass, which lies between the
two mountain ridges; and when we were near the

said entrance, on account of having to divide (the
force of) said soldiers, I asked the said Reverend
Father to give absolution to me and the said Army,
which he did, the greater part of them dismounting
from their horses, and then, when I reached the
said Pass, I again ordered them, through the said
interpreters, to demand once more that they should
deliver Our Lady and the Church Ornaments and the
captives as I (had) commanded yesterday evening,
and assured them, as I now assure them by repeated
requirement and exhortation, that I will pardon them
if they (will) come down to their villages like humble
vassals as they are of His Majesty, (and that) I will
return immediately, without doing harm to their
fields; and they, rebellious and traitorous, said they
did not want peace but war; and to incite their People to the said War, they made three fires, one above
on the summit of the ridge on the right hand sloping
to the said Pass, and two at the entrance and junc-
tion of the two ridges that separate and make an
opening to the said Pass; and I, said Govr. & Capt.
Genl., having conferred with the said Army Chiefs
and officers (in order) to arrange the manner of the
said engagement, taking into consideration and ad-
vantageous position in which the said enemy was
fortified in the said Pass, and their people distribu-
ted on the declivities of the said two ridges, so that
without being attacked, the mountains and rocks
themselves served as ramparts; and on our side, the
men being also ignorant (as to the character of) the
said entrance, therefore, the force was divided into
three divisions; the one at the entrance of the said

Pass was in charge of lieutenant governor and Capt. Genl. Maestro de Campo, Luis Granille, with the Captain of the Fort, Dn Antonio Valverde and some soldiers and half-pay officers and a part of the friendly Indians; and the other division, taking the side of the ridge on the left hand, was commanded by the Lieutenant General of Cavalry, Roque Madrid, and my Civil and Military Secretary and some soldiers and a part of the Indians of the friendly people, and the other ridge, on the right hand, I, said Governor and Captain General, commanded, with the Ensign Don Martin de Uriosette (of the said fort, and some soldiers and half-pay men and residents, and having gone up as far as they could, to scale the height of the said ridge and mounted the declivity to the summit, our men made themselves master of it, as did those under the Lieutenant-General of cavalry on the left side of said ridge, where he thought he had taken a position to dislodge the said enemy from it, because his division could stay there strengthening themselves and keeping the range, he might have, by repeated charges of firearms, and so the said lieutenant held his own, and those of the party on the ridge, while I took the right hand, seeing that those on the side of the said lieutenant general were continuing their fire in order to join the same section; they came down on foot by the said slope to the said Pass to see whether they were near the camp of the said enemy; and I, said Govr. and Capt. Genl., turned back to descend the said ridge and entered the said pass in all haste, in time to find the enemy already dislodged from their

WOOD FOR TAOS FIRES

Courtesy of F. T. Cheetham

said camp and scattered on the slopes of the said
two mountain ridges; and, because, as has been said,
the place was favorable to them, being so mountain-
ous and rocky, they succeeded in hiding and the
harm done them was through our men coming out
so loaded with clothing, skins of bulls and elk, big
and little, that many in order to keep the spoil, had
to dismount, leading the horses loaded with it, and
so, as the path in the said pass was very narrow, because there stood on the left hand the precipice of the
stream and the steep slopes of the two mountains,
and it was apparently about three quarters of a
league in length and terminated in a very high ridge,
from which there is no way out, and the place where
the said enemy had made their camp was a very
narrow spot, where, because they had cut down the
wood for the purpose of making their houses of logs
and rafters (morillos), which was the reason they
had chosen it and coming out in single file (alades
y lada) and very slowly from the said pass for the
reason aforesaid,—that the men were embarrased
with the spoils—the enemy repeated their shots from
the said ridge and wounded in the neck, with an arrow, the horse that I, said Govr. & Capt. Genl., was
riding in the advance; and also, as said Capt. Du
Antonio Balverde, remained in the rear-guard with
thirteen soldiers and retired officers and their ensign, the said Dn Martin de Uriosette, the said enemy
attacked them again; they came out at considerable
risk as the said ensign, also, had the sleeve on his
left arm pierced by an arrow, and one soldier came
out from the Pass wounded, and another with his

horse hurt; and from the side of the ridge on the left
hand, the enemy took the opportunity to attack the
horses of the Soldiers, aforesaid, who were with me,
said Govr. & Capt. Genl.; they came up and stole six
horses, leaving one soldier, who tried to defend himself, wounded, and, if my lieutenant, the Maestro de
campo, Luis Granillo, had not come up in time, they
would have taken the greater part of them; the said
enemy took the aforesaid opportunity on account of
the steepness of the mountain ridge, and my said
lieutenant being down at this spot, we divided our-
selves at different points, in order to get back the
said captures, only one soldier succeeding in regain-
ing a horse, wounding the said Indian who had stolen
it with a shot, and, on coming to the river and seeing
there were no more of the said enemies, I retired to
the said Village, which I had selected for headquarters, finding at the said barracks that the greater part of the said army had already arrived, all
highly pleased and giving thanks to God for such
a happy victory, at so little cost and loss, as it was,
though they must have been a major portion of the
said people (Indians), because the said enemy had
joined and united with the rebel nations, the Thanos
and the greater part of the Teguas, and some of the
Picuries, who came to help them; and it was reckoned
that four were killed, not counting many (who were)
wounded.   And in witness thereof, I signed this with
my Civil and Mil'y Sec'y.

Sept. 24, 1696.

On the twenty-fourth day of the month of September, of this date and year, I, said Govr. & Capt. Genl., seeing that the enemy still remained in force and vigor, because they had their horses, and the damages which had been done them was only the pillage of the goods taken from them found in their camp, and that they might have returned there and again united and set about its defense, when only four of them had been killed; for which reasons it was necessary to continue the War and by force of arms compel those who escaped with their lives to submit as vassals of his Majesty and beg for their lives, going back to reclaim their villages; and therefore, upon yesterday's experience, I again repeated the said order and manner of entrance into the Pass, which I effected together with the said Chiefs, giving the command of the ridge on the right to Commander Juan de Archuleta with his detachment and a portion of the friendlies, and to Adjt. Juan Ruiz de Cazares and sergeant Joseph Valdez, with commander Dn Ignazio de Roibal and his detachment and another portion of the Indian allies the ridge on the left hand; the aforesaid lieutenant general of cavalry not taking position among the rocks, as he did yesterday, but hunting on the left side for an entrance through the Mesa—looking for them on horseback over the highest part of the ridge; and I, said Govr. & Capt. Genl., having arrived, stayed at the mouth of the said Pass, giving time to the said Chiefs to mount the said ridges, and when they reached the summit, as has been said, I went in with the army

chiefs and my Civil and Mil'y Secretary, and we entered the said pass in perfect silence, and, having
reached the camp, we found that the enemy had not
slept there that night; and the said Captain Dn Antonio Valverde and his ensign, Don Marttin de Ur-
iostte, and likewise the said Lieutenant general of
cavalry, Roque Madrid, and some soldiers and retired officers, and a few friendly Indians went up to
the place where the said Adjutant Juan Ruiz was fir-
ing and discharging shots in order to arouse the
enemy who might be supposed to have just fled, in
order to destroy them if they were all together, by
cutting them in two and capturing some of them, and
the party go on by means of his declaration to rob
them of their horses; but neither one nor the other
party could capture anybody; they only recognized
the impregnable steepness of the mountain ridge, and
so they came down, remembering that they had left
me in the said Pass with a very small force and sus-
picious lest the enemy lie in ambush for me; and
when the said soldiers came back they discovered
many caves of the enemy, from which they again
robbed them of much booty in skins and furs, and
also the beans which they had already gathered from
the fields and dried; and they took the corn to dry in
the sun—the said men and their horses coming out
loaded with spoils aforesaid; and some Tegus Indian
woman came down and along with them an Indian
Sacristan named Felipe, and a Christian captive;
and they had collected some of the altar ornaments
and books of the Missionary Father which they had,
and also two coyote women who came down—Ida,

daughter of Geromilla, with her step-father named Joseph, bringing two little boys and two larger ones; and I left the said Pass without having suffered any misfortune and ordered many of the houses at the camp, in the said Pass, to be burned, returning to the said village and lodgings selected as headquarters; and in witness thereof and what occurred, I signed this with my Civil and Military Sec'y.

On the said day, month and year, at about four in the afternoon, the above mentioned Felipe, the Sacristan, being urged by me, said Govr. and Capt. Genl., with the kindest words, told me he would deliver the Blessed Virgin of Aranzazu, which he has hidden in his house, with some valuable altar ornaments of the Church, missals and books, and so I ordered the lieutenant general of cavalry and the magistrates and captains, Lazaro de Misquia and Diego Montoya, with a party of soldiers to go with him the said Indian, Phelipe, to his house, which is on the other side of the river, in the quarters of the Teguas as he is of that nation, and to bring Our Lady, aforesaid, as was due, and, therefore, I gave them the said detachment and some other persons who were of the said camp, chosen as excelling in Her Devotion, and they brought the said Blessed Image, the Commanders and Officers with the remainder of the said Men-at-Arms going out to receive Her, beyond the Parade Ground, and saluting with repeated shots from the Arquebuseers, and falling upon my knees, I received the said Image, which I took and placed in my tent. It is painted on a canvas about a yard and three quarters high and a quarter wide,

and the above mentioned Felipe delivered to me two
missals and an ornament, with all that belonged to
it, an alb and a censer of silver, with its large ladle,
and many books, and the box of holy oils, and, to en-
courage him, I embraced him, and made a feast for
him, so that, if anything was missing, he would bring
it forth; and he also handed over three candelabra
and the stamp he (father) had for making the wafer
(of the Host) and a bell and two hoods belonging to
the Father's wardrobe; and in witness thereof, I
signed this with my Civil and Military Sec'y.

Sept. 25, 1696.

On the twenty-fifth day of said month of September, this date and year, I said Govr. and Capt.
Gen'l., ordered the army to prepare to repeat the
said entry into the said Pass and carry out the work
of robbing the said enemy of their horses; and as
they were about to mount, and Cacique of the said
Village, Dn Bernardino, arrived, who had been
asked to come down by the said Indian, Jose, husband
of the Coyote, Geronima, and the aforesaid Phelipe,
Sacristan, and so, as he was reassured by the kindness I showed to the aforesaid who had surrendered,
as he could see, he came down without suspicion, and
so the said Geronima brought him into my tent, and
acting the part of interpreter, being well versed in
both languages, he told me that he came to ask that
they (my army) would do no damage to the fields
of his people; to which I replied that as long as they
delayed in submitting themselves as Vassals of His
Majesty, the people who entered into the said War

would receive that damage; that they had begun it,
saying that they did not want peace; and the army
would go on loading up with all that could be carried
away; and that he must go and say to his people that
they would see me pursuing them as long as they
were not in their said village, submitting like Vassals of His Majesty, as they are, and I would have
to kill, and order my soldiers to do likewise, and I
would also have to plunder all their goods and pro-
visions which they have hidden in the caves and
drying-platforms; that in order to see if the peace
they asked of me was sincere and not feigned for
the purpose of protecting their supplies, he must
bring the head of the Indian, Juan Griego, of the
Village of San Juan, since he told me that it was
for fear of him that they had arisen; and that this
was the reason that his said people of the said Village of San Juan were found with him; and that the
Thanos of the Village of San Cristobal were also
with them; and all of them had been in the fight of
the previous days, and all the said Cacique said was
that he would go and carry the said injunction to
his said people and come back to me again—if I
would see that their fields were not despoiled, to
which I replied: that those (fields) sowed by the
said Tegua and Thano enemies, who had made his
said people revolt—that these only would be despoiled by the said men of the said army of what was
needed by them, and so I told him to go; that I was
setting out for the Pass and elsewhere in search of
the said rebels, and the army officers and my lieutenant, seeing my resolution, told me they thought I

had better not go out while the said Cacique was carrying the said message, and that I ought to let such time elapse as I might think best to see whether or not they came down, and therefore, to save the lives of the two captive women they held: I told him they must bring or send them to me; that if it were not done today, I should go in search of them early tomorrow, and he promised me to send them, and, with considerable reluctance and hesitation, I gave up making the entrance and search for the said horses, but rather (in order) to save the lives of the said two captives by this means, and try the effect of the outcome of the said business and, in witness thereof, I signed this with my Civil and Military Secretary.

On the said day, month and year, the lieutenant of Govr. Pacheco, Dn Geronimo, came down and said that the reason the people had not come down was because they were scattered on the mountains, which was because they had heard many shots yesterday afternoon and (because) of the said Teguas having told them that the Spaniards were already killing the prisoners and that his people had scattered over the said mountains, because they were afraid, to which I replied by calling the said Indians, Phelipe, the Sacristan, and Jose and the others, and the said women, and I told him there they were—all alive— that the shots he said they had heard were rejoicing and salutation to Our Lady of Aranzazu, whom the said Indian, Phelipe, had delivered up; and that he must see what liars the said Teguas are; and how

THE SUN SYMBOL
Warren E. Rollins.

they deceived them in everything; I also said to the said lieutenant if the captive women were alive, why did he not bring them with him, and in a short time one came, the wife of the soldier, Juan de Mestas, who was brought by an Indian with whom the above mentioned Cacique, Dn Bernardino, sent her, and after the people who were going into the fields gathering corn had gone off, a woman came down from the mountain and, going to meet her, they saw that it was the other captive coming, named Catherine, wife of the settler, Phelipe Moraga, who was there and took her, and both the women came into my presence, dressed like Indians, with their hair cut short and told me the foregoing; and in witness thereof, I signed this with my Civil and Mil'y Sec'y.

On said day, month and year, at about five in the afternoon, as I was standing in the fields. which are in sight of the said Pass, where some of the men were with my lieutenant and also the lieutenant general of cavalry, Roque Madrid, I saw coming along the road leading from the Pass a troop of people, men, women and children, who were carrying loads, and when they were near enough I spoke to them and told them to have no fear; that I loved them all as my children, and it grieved me that they would not believe me, and that the troubles they had gone through on the mountains were from having believed tale-bearers (hatoleros) and I commanded them to go and take possession of the Houses they had, and to gather the supplies they had in the fields; whereup-on, immediately, they went well satisfied to live in

the said settlement of the Teguas; and in witness
thereof I signed this with my Civil and Military Secretary.

Oct. 2, 1696

On said day, the second of October, the said
Teguas having come down again and some families
of the Taos, I, said Govr. & Capt. Genl., having received them with all kindness; and also another troop
of families of the Teguas from the Village of San
Juan and of the Tanas (sic) and some Thaos who
were from the Villa of Santa fee, whom I had set
free at the end of the year 'ninety-four; and that
my wish for their reduction might be carried out, I
made the said lieutenant govr. of the said Pacheco
go to the mountains with two young braves of the
said Taos who had come down; that he should go
with them and tell the said Pacheco, his Govr., and
his people, that they must come down to their village, with the assurance that nobody should harm
them; that they would be received in the same way
that those who were now there had been received;
and this was said in the most convincing words (in
order) to remove their suspicions, aforesaid, giving
all of them a feast; and he went away well content
with the said young braves, saying that he could not
return until the following day in the afternoon, because it had snowed hard, and they (the Indians)
were scattered all over the mountains where he would
have to hunt for them; and in witness thereof, I
signed with my said Civil and Military Sec'y.

Oct. 3, 1696

On said day, the third of October of this date
and year, at about six in the evening, there came into my presence Governor Pacheco, of this said Village of Taos, with his said lieutenant, sent yesterday
by me, said Govr. & Capt. Genl., with the message
certified in these edicts, and he told me through the
Coyote Indian, Geronima, who acted as interpreter,
that he came into my presence that I might do what
I pleased with him; that he had said this to his
people; that he was going down to submit, even if
they took his life—as the rebel Tegua and Thanos
Indians had said, and that with all the quarrels they
were having and the mischievous lies they were
spreading and talking, they were perishing of hun-
ger and dying of cold on the mountains; and that on
the fourth day they were about to come down, when
a Navajo Apache came to them, with a message from
the rebel Gemes, saying that they must not believe
me; that I would take the lives of all of them; and
they, therefore, should not come down seeking peace
for which reason the said people had scattered all
over the mountain in fear; and that he holds as prisoners three Thanos Indians to bring down to me, because they are those who, by their bad advice, had
made his said people revolt as well as the Indian,
Juan Griego, of whom they have great fear, and
everybody in the village of the San Juan Teguas
obeys him; and they also are in favor of the said
Thanos because they are numerous and brave, as
were also the said Teguas; and that the said three
Tanos whom he has imprisoned tell him they are

carrying you (plural) off so that you shall die at
the same time with us; it is for this that the said
Govr. & Capt. Genl. sends for you, though you say
he is your friend; you will see down there that he is
a poor miserable (friend) to you; and when the said
Apache came he was afraid and set them at liberty;
and they fled immediately with some others who were
with them on the said mountain and carried off some
horses stolen from them; and that upon the information he had from the two young braves who went with
his lieutenant and the message they give him and
told him with what satisfaction the said Teguas were
living, gathering in their supplies, as well as the Teguas and Thanos who had come down, and that all
had been pardoned, he came down resolved to die;
and therefore, I might do with him as I pleased; that
he had done no wrong in the Church; that Juan Griego and the said Thanos had taken the keys from him
and put the horses in it, and that the reason for their
having made it into a stable was because they had
put the forge in there, which seemed to them not so
great a sin as the first, all of which, through the said
Coyote, Geronima, he declared and told at great
length; therefore, I said to him he must inform me of
everything that he might have to say; and he said
that the Teguas and Juan Griego had eaten all the
sheep belonging to the Father; and that there was
only a horse which had been left for him to keep,
which he delivered, and the Reverend Father Fray
Blas Navarro, chaplain of the said army, received it;
it was a red chestnut and was recognized as belonging to their Reverend Father, who was Reverend

JUANITA.
Catharine C. Critcher

Fray Antonio Carboneli, whom the Thanos Indians
of San Cristobal killed in company with their own
priest, Fray Joseph de Arbizu, on the fourth of June
at sunset on the day of their rising, and thereupon,
I told him he must now try only to bring them down
to their said Village, where they must live submis-
sive as Vassals of His Majesty; and that for Christians, as they were, I was ashamed of them; that they
had revolted to their own will and from believing, as
he says the stories told them by the said Teguas and
Juan Griego, and the Thanos, and that neither I, nor
the Spaniards had done them any harm, nor are we
doing anything for which they should rebel, since I,,
on my part asked nothing of them and took nothing
from them, neither did the Spaniards acquiesce in or
do them any harm whatever; and that which was
done in the light on the first day, I had demanded of
them in peace; and that they had begun the fight not-
withstanding which, the second day, I returned to
treat with them of the said peace and they had replied that they did not want peace but war; and that
I, out of pity, had left them necessary stores in their
said fields besides what they had hidden in their drying-platforms and caves of the said Pass and mountain, as well as much clothing, and, in order that they
should not be robbed of it, I had not gone on doing it;
that they also had all their horses and I only commanded them to return the horses which were our
own, and the firearms they have, for which purpose
I ordered him to go back to the said mountain and
bring down his said people, and he should tell them
what I had said, assuring them that no harm would

be done to them; and he repeated that no more of their corn ought to be gathered, to which I said two things; the first, that until they should come down the people who had come with me to the said war would go and take what was needed; the second, that only by my orders would they keep their fields and they might have charge of those of the said rebels who have done their sowing—the Teguas and Thanos—and with this I dismissed him, treating him with much kindness, he telling me that he would go to the said mountain on the following day, but on account of the deep snow, and the said people being much scattered, three or four days would be needed to gather his people and return with those he might induce to come; and seeing that on this day the said Lieut. Gen'l. of Cavalry had set out with five days grace, it would be necessary to warn the supply train which might be much embarrassed if the said people were coming down at once, I gave him not only the aforesaid time that he asked, but told him that he said well; that however slowly he gathered in his said people, I should be satisifed; that I was not in a hurry; that I would wait for them, and so the aforesaid took his leave, and in witness thereof, I made affidavit which I signed, with my said Civil and Military Sec'y.

Oct. 7, 1696

On the seventh day of the month of October, of this date and year, the Lieutenant general of Cavalry, Roque Madrid, arrived, having delivered the relief supplies sent to the Villa Nueva of Santa Cruz,

which I sent there on the third, and with which he left
it provisioned until the end of November; and he
said that in passing the Village of Picuries he took
prisoner the wife and daughter of Dn Anttonio, the
Picuris Cacique, brother of Dn Lorenzo, the Governor, and an Indian woman, all of whom were in
the fields, and (that) the Indian men who were with
them fled to the ravine; and he also took with these
an old woman, who was the mother of the said wife
of Dn Anttonio, aforesaid, and he thought best to
send her, as he did the said old woman, to tell the
said people who are with Dn Lorenzo and Dn Anttonio, aforesaid; on the mountain, that they must
come down submissively to their said village; that
he assured them that I would pardon them, as I had
done the Thaos people, who are now in said Village,
and the wife and daughter would likewise be returned to him and the other Indian woman whom he
was taking to the Villa Nueva de Santa Cruz, where
they would remain until they should have come down
and seen me passing through the said Village; and
the old woman, aforesaid, promised to take and deliver to them the aforesaid (message) which she was
made to understand throroughly by the mouth of Matias Lujan, soldier of the Garrison of the Villa of
Canta Fee, who acted as interpreter; and, on his return he had likewise talked with the two Indians,
and told them the same thing; and he brought to me
the nephew of the said Dn Anttonio that I might talk
to him; and he being in my presence, I treated him
kindly and told him the aforesaid, which he must
repeat to his said people, with which he was content,

and I also told him the aforesaid, which he must repeat and I also told him that he must tell them that
when they came down together, they must bring me
the altar ornaments of the Church, and other things
they might have belonging to the Father and the said
Indian is a son of Don Luis (Tupatu), the deceased
Picuris, who was an elder brother of the said Dn
Lorenzo and Dn Anttonio; it was he who was govern-
ing all this Kingdom in the year 'ninety-two, when I
conquered it to my cost; and in witness of the said
arrival and information, I signed this with my said
Military and Civil Sec'y.

On said day, month and year, as dated, the said
Governor Pacheco came down from the mountain
bringing in his company the greater part of his people, with their chusma, and loaded with their posses-
sions; whereupon I went out to receive them on the
parade ground and talked to them with words of
great kindness, affection and tenderness, and embraced the women and children, and I told them also
that they should go and live in their Houses, which,
for this purpose, I had ordered the men of said army
to abandon and they went with visible pleasure; and
the said Pacheco also brought two of the horses
which were stolen on the day of the fight, which
were recognized by the soldiers, who were their own-
ers, and were ordered delivered to them; and he said
that of the others which were missing three had been
taken by the said Thanos the night that they (the
Tanos) stole theirs, and that in gathering together
their horses, not only those that were missing but
those that they knew did not belong to the said In-

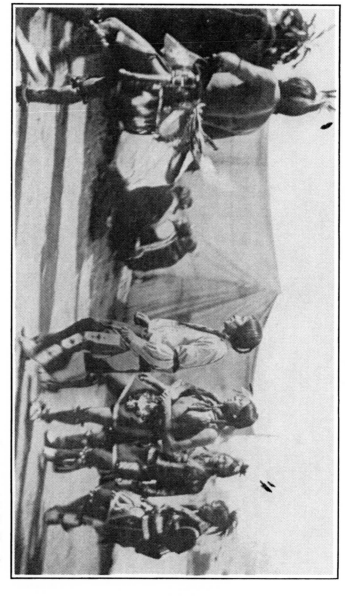

TAOS INDIANS DANCING TO THE SINGING OF THE DRUMMERS.

Courtesy of F. T. Cheetham

dians would be sent and delivered to me; and I repeated to him also that the firearms they had must
be likewise delivered and required him to make haste
with that matter and advise me of everything; and I
told him he might go and rest and we would talk tomorrow if God pleased; and in testimony thereof, I
signed this with civil and military sec'y.

Oct. 8, 1696

On the eighth day of the month of October, of
this day and year, I said Govr. & Capt. Genl., summoned the said Govr. Pacheco and his lieutenant
and other chiefs, with their interpreter, Juan, a Tegua Indian, and commanded him, seeing that the
Church had been deprived of its stockade, and it not
fit to use, having had a stable and a forge in it, to
order all the people to tear it down at once; to sweep
and clean up the said place, and on the Mesa where
the Altar stood, and where they have adobe, they
must plant a Cross before which and on said spot his
said People shall pray; and they went off immediately to order done what I had commanded and instructed them to do.   In testimony whereof, I signed this
with my civil and military Sec'y.

Oct. 9, 1696

On the ninth day of the month of October of this
day and year, I, said Govr. and Capt. Genl., the said
People of the Tiguas and the greater part of the
Thaos, being already in their quarters, and their
Govr., lieutenant, war-captains and other chiefs having begged me, in view of the fact that so many persons, the Indians as well as the soldiers and others

connected with the said camp, require great supplies,
for pity's sake to retire and leave them the freedom
of their village in order that their fields may not be
entirely consumed; that the people who have failed to
come down are searching for and guarding the horses
of all of them, and also of the clothing they had to
protect themselves with on the mountain, aforesaid,
and I, said Govr. & Capt. Genl. seeing that the people of the said Army were a charge upon them, gave
them to understand the mercy I showed them in leaving them such abundant supplies, and that I would
go; and I commanded them to live as loyal vassals
of His Majesty; and that while the Frayle who
wished to minister to them was coming, they must
say the Prayers for evening, morning and midday before the Holy Cross they had planted; and they said
they would take care and fulfill all that I commanded
them; and I told them they must go and join their
said people on the said site of the said church; and
when they were together the Father Chaplain of the
said Army would go, as I asked him to do, and give
them absolution for their apostasy; and the said
Army being already prepared and the pack train
having set out, which I ordered loaded for the third
journey that it made to the Villa of Santa Fee, I
raised the siege, setting out from said Parade
Ground with the detachment of soldiers which I had
taken to escort the said Army with which I went to
the site where the said Church had been and found
the people gathered and the said Father Chaplain
was just finishing absolving that they should say
their prayers, morning and evening and at midday,

like the Christians they were; that they must not
trust anymore the talebearers; and I gave orders to
their Govr., lieutenant and War-captains in their
presence that whosoever should come to them with a
bad talk, in order not to risk his escaping from them
by the way they must kill him and bring me his head;
and in order to call the people to prayer at the hours
of the day, I told them they must hand the bell they
had, since it should also be of use to them if their
enemies should come in, for by striking it they could
find out whether there were any Spaniards in their
company; and I also told them they must come to
see me and report at the Villa Santa fee, so that I
should hear of them and of all their enemies; and I
took leave of them with all kindness and affection,
which I showed by giving them my hand and em-
bracing them and telling them they were my children;
and I went on with the said Army to sleep at the
post of Miranda, a distance of four leagues, where I
arrived before sunset; and in witness thereof I
signed this with my Civil and Military Secy.

During this visit of De Vargas, it seems the
church was ruined because he used it as a stable. It
was then razed to the ground and the foundation
cleaned. So it is very probable that the church of
which only the ruins now stand was built about 1704[21]
instead of 1632 as often given. After its destruction
in 1847 at the order of Col. Price, the Indians chose

21. This is the date which Col. R. E. Twitchell suggests.

again the oldest site of all[22] on which to build their present small chapel.

*   *   *   *   *   *

During the following fifty years, the Taos Indians seemed to have had a change of heart and became friendly with the whites. They seem to have learned to understand better what these new men might do in the way of protecting them from their enemies, especially the Commanches who had suddenly appeared about 1714 after a long journey of twelve moons and were bent on fighting everybody. The Taos seem to have welcomed all the Spanish explorers after 1700, that year in which they encouraged the Navajo to make peace with the Spaniards at the Taos pueblo.

In 1706 Uribarri came through Taos bent on capturing and bringing back runaway Picuries Indians who had followed the trail of the Taos who had fled some years before. In 1719, Gov. Valverde started out to punish Utes and Commanches and he too, with Taos allies no doubt, for he claimed to have had 495 Indians and Mexican servants with his group of 105 Spaniards when he left Taos. He like the others went east "along Fernando Creek"[23] or through our Taos Cañon and then on over the mountains.

The next year 1720, Don Pedro de Villasur, who had been with the other two expeditions, was given

---

22. According to the Indians.
23. Spanish Expeditions into Colorado—Alfred B. Thomas. Colo. State Hist. Society Publication—1924.

orders to find out more about the Frenchmen to the east, who were considered more dangerous enemies of the Spaniards than the wild tribes of Indians. He came through Taos and then followed that eastward trail where he eventually lost his life in his "camp in the tall grass" where Pawnees surrounded all the party. Eleven men came back to get fresh horses left in Taos and tell of the death of their comrades, among whom were probably many Taos braves.

These days of the early and middle part of the eighteenth century were the days of the successful summer fairs at our pueblo. Spaniards came from far away Chihuahua. Indians came from everywhere and always among them were the trouble making Commanches.

Finally a junta was held in 1748 or 9 in Santa Fé to see what should be done about these rascally Indians. Junta or no, they still came to the fairs and though the Spaniards knew there was always danger of a general massacre, they lived on separated, as they were all over the valley, believing they could make good no doubt in case of any serious uprising. Such, however, was not the case. In 1760, a Commanche chief with his war braves came down from the mountains to demand the young daughter of the Spaniard Pando who had years before been promised to him. She refused to go with the chief. A wild war whoop crashed on the air, probably along the road now leading to the village of Cañon since. the Indians say, the houses of the Spaniards were on the ground now occupied by the Couse and Sharp studios. Men defended their beloved ones in vain. Fifty women at least, were seized and swung on the horses of their captors. Then, stained with much blood, these Commanches urged on their horses. They passed to the south and east of the Taos pueblo and went on into the foothills to the north, singing as they went. The Indian of today knows the story well and one recently said, "They even know the song they were singing as they went."

Right here it would be well to pause to read several paragraphs written by Bishop Tamaron[24] who visited Taos in 1760 and while his story may be wrong in some details, he must have heard of this fight first hand. His account of the pueblo itself is also of interest and begins,

"To reach this Indian pueblo, whose patron saint is San Gerónimo one traveled over pine covered mountains until making the descent to the spacious and beautiful valley called Taos; in which were encountered villages of peaceable heathen Apaches, who are gathered under the protection of the Spaniards for defense against the Commanches. Then a river was encountered which they call Las Trampas, which has a good flow of water. Half a day was spent in a large house of a rich Indian of Taos, very intelligent and well off. His house and lands are surrounded by (armas) for defense. In the afternoon the journey was continued through that valley. Three rivers were crossed, of the same current and

---

24. Village tradition says the most desperate battle took place near the site of the present Harwood studio. This is what was remembered by Teresina Bent Scheurich, the most reliable of all old-timers in Taos.
       Through the courtesy of Dr. H. E. Bolton of Berkeley, a translation of this letter was made recently by Nellie V. Sanchez·

amount of water as the first; all have plenty of water for irrigating and are distant from one another about a league and a half. After passing the last one, the pueblo of Taos was entered, where a Franciscan missionary curate resides. It is 12 leagues distant from Picuries to the north, and is the last and most retired pueblo of that kingdom in this direction. It is situated at the foot of a very high mountain range, in 40 degrees. This pueblo has 159 Indian families numbering 505 persons, and has as neighbors 36 white families numbering 160 persons. It has a very good, capacious church.

This pueblo is divided into three sections with many stories and it would be better, as I told them, if they had a common door; for one of them is on the other side of the river, and about 200 yards from the crossing of the river. It has a wooden bridge and it freezes over every year. When it is thus frozen up, they told me, the Indian women came with their children, naked, broke the ice with a stone and bathed them in those waters, putting them in and taking them out. They say it is done so they may become hard and strong.

While I was in this pueblo two villages of friendly, but heathen Ute Indians arrived with a captive, who fled from the Commanches. They said the Commanches remained on the Las Animas River hunting buffalo, in order to come to the fairs; every year they come to the fairs. The governor comes with a great part of his presidio and people from all over the kingdom to those fairs, which they call ransoms. They bring captives to sell, buckskins, many buffalo

hides and booty that they have taken in other parts—
horses, guns, muskets, ammunition, knives, meat and
various other things. No money circulates in these
fairs but articles are traded for each other and in
this way those people provide for themselves.

"I left Taos on June 12 and a few days afterward 17 tents of Commanches arrived. They make
these tents of buffalo skins and they say they are
good and a fine protection, each one being occupied
by a family. At the end of the said month of June 70
of these field tents arrived, making the big fair............

"On the 6th of August, there came in war, so
they say, nearly 3000 Commanche men. with the in-
tention of making an end of this pueblo of Taos.
They (the people of Taos) attacked and provoked
them from a very large house, the largest in all the
valley, belonging to an Indian called Villapando, who
luckily for him, went away that day on business that
came up. Seeing so many Commanches coming, because this house was the strongest, many women and
men of that neighborhood took refuge in it, trust-
ing in the circumstance that that house had four
towers, and a large provision of muskets, powder
and ball. It is said that they fired on them.

"At this the Commanches became infuriated to
such a horrible extent that they broke down the house
in several places and killed all the men and some of
the women, who also fought. The mistress of the
house, seeing that they were breaking in the outside
door, taking up a lance went to defend it and they
killed her fighting, 56 women and children were carried off and a large number of ' horses which the

THE CIRCLE DANCE
As given at the Santa Fe Fiesta, 1925.

Courtesy of El Palacio

owner of the house had there. Of the Commanches
49 dead bodies were counted and others running
blood.

"The governor Don Francisco Marin del Valle,
as soon as he learned of the affairs, convoked the
people as rapidly as possible and setting out with a
thousand men on their trail, followed them almost
200 leagues, when the Apaches, being tired and the
food giving out, lost heart and returned. 40 days
were spent in this, in which they explored good
country but accomplished nothing else."

Before we leave the early eighteenth century it
will be of interest to know how the mission at the
Pueblo was faring. Bishop Crespo of the Catholic
Church visited New Mexico and wrote, upon his return to Spain, a "Memorial" in which he accused,
among others, Padre Juan Mirabal of Taos of neg-
lecting his duties. He made sweeping accusations
that the priests would not learn the Indian language
and the Indians in turn would not confess through
an interpreter. He declared that tithes were not
properly collected and deplored the sort of lives
many of the priests were leading. The accusations
were based too solidly on fact to be refuted so the
priests rose with their only countercharge that the
governors were abusing the Indians and making
them work without pay. Neither government officials nor priests were trying to give the Indians a
square deal. That is only too evident.

During the next few years there were several
priests who came to Taos probably to investigate
matters. Don Juan de Ordenal in 1750 made a trip

into New Mexico. As layman and businessman he seconded all that Bishop Crespo had written and advised secularization. This, of course, made the priests angry but to no avail as they could not refute the charges. Secularization did not come for about seventy-five years though there is no reason to believe the priests changed much in their lives.

The following reports made by priests who came to visit Taos and refused to see what Bishop Crespo had been too daring not to see, are of interest, however ,and lend color to the life of that day in the pueblo.

In 1744, Father Menchero wrote of the pueblo as follows:

"Taos—The Mission of Taos the last to the north and the place where Christianity ends is thirty leagues from the Capital and seven hundred from Mexico City where, I, the witness, went and visited at the cost of immense work. This very charming pueblo has one hundred seventy families and is located at the foot of a steep mountain from which flows three rivers which water a pleasing valley. At a distance of three leagues all three come together and in one league more they empty into the Rio Grande del Norte.

Two priests serve in this pueblo for the administration of the Holy Sacraments and for the political government an alcalde mayor is appointed by the Governor of the Kingdom because it is the most populous settlement on the entry way of the barbarians who come to exchange the captives which they bring to sell."

Ten years later, in his cell in the convent of San Matias de Istacalo Fray Manuel de San Nepomuceno y Trigo wrote of our pueblo the following interesting paragraphs.

"This Mission is the last in this Holy Custodia, twelve leagues north from Picuries and is the first one to which most of the tribes come together for their fairs which are governed by the moon and which the Governor of the Kingdom and his lieutenant governor attends with many vecinos and soldiers. The Indians sow four fanegas of wheat in the valley and a cuartila of maize, from the harvest of which the Father has bread all year. They give him two boys for the cell, a cell ringer, a porter, two sacristans, a cook, all the wood which is need and two women to grind the wheat.

"This and all the other missions which have Indians and are composed of them gather in the village in this manner: at seven in the morning the girls meet in the church at the ringing of the bell, where the minister, with the fiscal present, recites with them all the prayers and the catechism. They close with a hymn which is pleasing enough and they go to their homes. The boys do the same and the rest of the town recites the prayer in the same way, only on Sundays they say it after Mass while the Father eats his breakfast so that he may go on with his duties."[25]

*　　*　　*　　*　　*　　*

25. Translation by Ettie M. Healy in "The New Mexico Missions in the Middle Eighteenth Century." Berkeley University.

About 1825, there came to Taos a man by the name of George C. Yount who presumably joined trapping expeditions led by Ewing Young and was also for a time one of the party of which the Patties were members if not leaders. Later he told the tale of his wanderings to Rev. Orange Clark who wrote it down as Yount told it about 1851, out in California. He spoke of knowing many Indians of the southwest, among them, the Taos. Here is what he said of our Indians:[26]

The Taos Indian.

"The Taos Indians have their town, or cluster of towns at the foot of a lofty chain of mountains— The dwellings are erected in long blocks, five stories high, and are intended, not only for dwellings, but for fortifications—They have no entrance except on the roof by a trap-door. They ascend on rude ladders capable of being drawn up and laid upon the roof. Here they are afforded a secure retreat from their enemies, the Eutaus, Comanches, Apaches and others. It is a remarkable fact that, although the Spaniards who have settled around them and multiplied ever since they overran the country are corrupt to the last degree, so that chastity among the female sex is almost unknown, yet these Indians hold sacred the marriage rite, and nothing is more rare among them than an unchaste woman—No impurity or immorality is tolerated or has ever been. Their sacrifice fire has always been kept burning. This fire is in a cell under ground, and a certain number of boys

26. Cal. Hist. Society Quarterly—Vol. 2, No. 1. "The Chronicles of George C. Yount" by Charles L. Camp.

are selected at an early age[27] and promoted to the
honorable distinction of feeding this fire—These
youths remain at their post day and night until they
reach a certain age when they are brought out to
light and carried to the top of the loftiest mountain
to remain there during a fixed series of years, and
others take their place at the fire. Their females
are exceedingly beautiful. The men are brave and
warlike. Once every year they go on a general hunt
for Buffalo meat in the north and at other seasons
they are often employed by the Spaniards to guard
them in *their* hunting and trapping excursions. They
have a tradition[28] that all that part of the Globe
about where they dwell was anciently devastated,
how and by what means they can not tell: and that
when their people came nine white men held the
country—four of which were slain, and five fled, and
wandered off towards the north—and that their own
people came from the setting sun—Underground, far
beneath the surface are extensive excavations and the
ruins of ancient palaces: in one of which is the Holy
Fire above described—The above named Chief John
God,[29] during his intimacy, informed Y(oun)t that
when the Spaniards overran the country the Gold
and Silver in the nation was thrown into a large lake
which lies near the centre of their territory, lest it
might excite their cupidity & lead them to search
more diligently for the mines of precious metals,
which are very rich & abundant & are kept secreted

27. Here Yount refers to the "religious education" as it is known
    today. Note the mention of the fire sacred to Po-so-yemo or
    Montezuma.
28. This tradition still holds at the pueblo. It probably links up with
    the story of the flood told them by the Spaniards.
29. This name Juan de Dios is a familiar one among Taos Indians.

to this day—So cautious are they from generation to generation that where the silver appears above ground, they visit it, after every rain, to cover it, in case the water have washed off the surface—earth— This Chief (John God) during their intimacy, had arranged to conduct Yount to these mines but the intimacy, had excited the jealousy of the Council of Chiefs & they took him into the Council room & informed him of their suspicions & assured him, that, if he should betray the secret, they would take the life of both him & Y(oun)t. The Chief did not venture therefore to do more than point in the direction & describe the spot & Y(oun)t has never ventured to explore or prospect for the mines.''[30]

Life now went on fairly serenely save possibly for some skirmishes with wandering wild Indians for it was not until about 1868 that the government moved these Indians to reservations some two hundred miles away.

The last appearance of the wild tribes in the valley was some time in the thirties. They seem to have stolen in unnoticed by the sentinel high up on the mountain. No warning fire put men on the watch. So cattle and horses were being driven off. Col. José Valdez, who had won his reputation as a great

30. The story of "good rocks" far up the mountain is still told. The Indians even go so far as to say there is an altar of solid gold on the mountainside. They believe they will lose their homes if they ever allow the white man to open up mines on their land, yet this is their one way to wealth.

One young Indian, found bringing down specimens of rock on burros, was severely reprimanded by the old men and his burros taken from him about twenty years or more ago.

Another Indian carries with him today a good specimen of silver and demands ten dollars of those who wish to find the place where he says he found the rock. He has taken more than one man into the cañon only to be unable to find the place. Then he comes to town and boasts of how much he has made with that one stone.

Indian fighter undertook to give these Indians a lesson. With a small party including some Taos Indians undoubtedly, he followed the trail through the
Rio Chiquito Cañon, then up over the hill where the
men dropped down to the trail in Taos Cañon. Here
they quickly felled great trees and piled brush.
Along came the rascals unaware of danger ahead.
Then came a sharp fight and ''Mr. Indian Thieves
were severely punished,'' said an old timer who added, ''I never heard of wild Indians in here again,
though the plains Indians made raids after that.''

Meantime, the Spaniards were slowly outnum-
bering the Indians and they were finally asked by
them to move a league away, so their story runs, and
then came the enlargement of the settlement of Don
Fernando de Taos to the south in 1796. Life in the
pueblo and in the town seems to have been fairly
akin. There was little in the way of class distinction
apparently. Finally a Catholic Church was established during the early years of the nineteenth century and life in Taos became much less like that of
the Indians, who adhered to their old-time customs
and gave their age-old dances while attending to the
church made for them by the Spaniards.

*   *   *   *   *   *

Now came the days of the wagons from the east.
Traders of all classes were as welcome in town as at
the pueblo as far we know. Taos Indians acted as
look-outs along the trail and undoubtedly helped
build those fires down on this side of the flat-topped

mountain to the east of town, which warned the citizens that hostile Indians were on the path of the coming white men in the stage.

Taos Indians acted as guides, hunters and friends of the white man. There is still living at the pueblo an Indian Mauricio Martinez, who, in his youth, was sought by a Taos man.[31]. A message of some great import must go east to Westport Landing (Kansas City) and he was chosen as the most reliable scout. Wandering by streams, up over rocky mountains he took his course afoot. Careful of crunching leaves or fallen twigs, he denied himself comforting fire by night after he had seen "signs." His quick eye caught sight of soft moccasin marks in the sand or forest mold. He could tell what tribe had passed by, whether they were bent on war or peace and whither they were going. Then silently, he bent his course accordingly, on, on alone over the hundreds of miles he went, with his message, to the city of the white man. It was as daring and splendid a journey as any ever made by white men of the early west.

It is a great pity that more stories of brave Taos Indians have not been written down. We believe there were many worthy of a faithful scribe's attention. One of these which was so notable that it forced attention, I have chosen to give. It is found in the account of one of the early wagon trains which came to Taos and Santa Fé and then went on its weary miles of trail back east. Of this eastward journey we have the following:

31. Pascual Martinez.

THE DAYS OF THE WAGONS.
Centenary Celebration Train from Cañon, Sept. 29, 1925.

Courtesy of Olive Baxter

"The return caravan (in 1829) was escorted to the Arkansas by Mexican troops commanded by Colonel Viscara. While in the valley of the Cimarron they were attacked by the Indians; Cooks says by Arapahoes and Commanches; Gregg says Gros Ventros. A party of about one hundred and twenty Indians approached on foot. The traders were opposed to admitting them to camp near. He promised the traders that the Indians should be disarmed, but they were too sharp for him and most of them retained their weapons. When an opportune moment arrived they sprang up with a frightful yell and commenced the attack. They seemed especially bent on killing the Mexican commander, and one of the chiefs, when only a few feet away, leveled his gun to fire. A Taos Indian, one of the Colonel's body-guard, seeing his master in danger, sprang in between him and the chief and received the contents of the gun in his own heart. A brother of this Indian sprang like a tiger at the chief and slew him on the spot. An officer and two of the soldiers were killed but none of the traders were injured. The latter joined with the troops in repulsing the attack, which was easily accomplished, after which the Indians were relentlessly pursued and killed wherever overtaken. It is said that the pursuers displayed true savage barbarity in the vindictive way in which they wreaked vengeance upon those Indians and that they went back to the States with human scalps dangling to their horses' bridles."[32]

32. Chittenden—Vol. II. Page 511-512. History of the American Fur Trade in the Far West.

There is a charming story written about 1846 or
7 by that soldier wanderer George Frederick Ruxton
about a trip through the Gila country when a friendly Taos was among the party. They came upon the
ruined walls of the homes of long-forgotten Indians.
They turned up to the light bits of old pottery,
jewelry, arrow heads and roamed thoughtfully
through the broken walls.

"A Taos Indian, who was amongst the band,
was evidently impressed with a melancholy awe",
says Ruxton,[33] "as he regarded these ancient monuments of his fallen people. At midnight he rose from
his blanket and left camp which was in the vicinity
of the ruined city, stealthily picking his way through
the line of slumbering forms which lay around and
the watchful sentinel observed him approach the
ruins with a slow and reverential gait. Entering the
moldering walls, he gazed silently around where in
ages past his ancestors trod proudly, a civilized race,
the tradition of which, well-known to his people, served but to make their present degraded position
more galling and apparent. Cowering under the
shadow of a crumbling wall, the Indian drew his
blanket over his head and conjured to his mind's eye
the former power and grandeur of his race—that
warlike people who, forsaking their own country for
causes of which no tradition, however dim, now ex-
ists, sought in the fruitful and teeming valleys of the
south a soil and climate which their own lands did not
afford, and, displacing the wild and barbarous

---

33. "In the Old West"—G. F. Ruxton.

hordes inhabiting the land, raised there a mighty empire, great in riches and civilization.

The Indian bowed his head, and mourned the fallen greatness of his tribe. Rising, he slowly drew his tattered blanket round his body and prepared to leave the spot when the shadow of a moving figure, creeping past a gap in the ruined wall through which the moonbeams played, suddenly arrested his attention. Rigid as a statue, he stood transfixed to the spot, thinking a former inhabitant of the city was visiting in a ghostly form, the scenes his body once knew so well. The bow in his right hand shook with fear as he saw the shadow approach, but was as tightly and steadily grasped when, on the figure emerging from the shade of the wall, he distinguished the form of a naked Apache, armed with bow and arrow, crawling stealthily through the gloomy ruins.

Standing undiscovered within the shadow of the wall, the Taos raised his bow and drew an arrow to the head, until the other who was bending low to keep under cover of the wall and thus approached the sentinel, standing at a short distance, seeing suddenly the well-defined shadow on the ground, rose upright on his legs, and, knowing escape was impossible, threw his arms down his sides, and drawing himself erect exclaimed in a suppressed tone, 'wagh'!

'Wagh', exclaimed the Taos likewise but quickly dropped his arrow point and eased the bow.

'What does my brother want,' he asked, 'that he lopes like a wolf round the fires of the white hunters?'

"Is my brother's skin not red?" returned the

Apache, ''and yet he asks question that need no answer. Why does the medicine-wolf follow the buffalo and deer? For blood—and for blood the Indian follows the treacherous white from camp to camp, to strike blow for blow, until the deaths of those so basely killed are fully avenged.''

'My brother speaks with a big heart, and his words are true; and though the Taos and Pimo (Apache) black their faces towards each other (are at war), here, on the graves of their common fathers, there is peace between them. Let my brother go.'

The Apache moved quickly away, and the Taos once more sought the campfires of his white companions.''

THE PUEBLO CHURCH RUINS, 1925.

Courtesy of H. E. High

PART II.

1847—

Dates now bring us to the year 1847 when there occurred the revolution in Taos. Priests from the south had done their best to stir up feeling against the Americans among the Indians and Mexicans. The Indians declared that their leader Tomasito did not want to join in the revolt but that later under the influence of American whiskey he with his group did so. It is quite true that whiskey played the villian's part in this insurrection. Neither Indian nor Mexican fight unless under great pressure or under the influence of liquor. This brought sorrow to the Indian pueblo for their men were hung for the murder of Governor Bent and others in town. Perhaps they too thought that if once the town could be cleared of Americans, the place would again be solely theirs. That is known to have been the thought of some of the mob. This they were to learn could not be ever again. Few Indians came to town and no women from the pueblo during the year following the trouble in town.

Of the battle at the pueblo much has been written. The Indians say that Col. Price's men were all drunk but they managed to storm the old church and, also, ruin it. On its top many Indians gathered and placed their guns. One Mexican woman, Pin Dassa, the wife of "Big Nigger" the Delaware who fought so valiantly within the church, was on the top and help load the guns.

Finally below, in spite of all ''Big Nigger'' could do in the way of holding back the door, the hinges gave. Despair entered with the Americans. An old Indian who told of being in the fight, said, ''Indian, Indian, he like prairie dog'' and pawing the air tried to show how the red men in their fight made frantic efforts to dig themselves into the hard mud floor of the church.

Apparently every possible effort of all adult Indians was thrown into this last fight with the American. They claim the Mexicans deserted and ran and left the brunt of the battle to them. However that may be, it was the last time the Taos Indian ever tried real battle.

Very soon after these days of trouble in 1847, we find this record which surely does credit to our Indians and should be quoted.

[34]''The Indians have been coming in and seemed pleased at the new order of things; temporary civil officers have been sworn in. The authorities of Taos have submitted and the prefect taken oath of allegiance. Some of the civilized or ''Pueblo'' Indians from that quarter have visited us. These are a remarkable element in the New Mexican population. They are of the full blood, live in villages of many stories[35] without doors—enter each story from its top which is reached by movable ladders; their diligently cultivated grounds they hold in fee; they speak the Spanish, besides an original language;

34. Philip St. George Cook—1847—Col. Cooke was with the army of the west under Gen. Kearney.
35. The northern pueblo is now five stories; the southern only four. There are many other houses near. About 600 Indians are now living.

comparatively moral, they profess the Roman Catholic religion slightly modified by some cherished customs and ceremonies but are reputed far more moral Christians than the New Mexicans proper, that is, of mixed blood; of these, the priests being preeminent scoundrels. Their flocks are generally earnest in an imitation where their inferior means and abilities do not admit of a possible success.''

* * * * * *

Before we write of the Indian as he is today, it would be well to speak here of the problem of lands and water since the subject has recently been frequently discussed in the press.

As far as the Taos Indian is concerned his grant of land has not been much altered since the U. S. Government took over the southwest. On Dec. 22, 1858, Congress confirmed the old land grant in which the King of Spain gave a league square to each pueblo, amounting to practically two and one-half miles from the church in all directions. No titles were given to Indians in severalty and no Indian could, in consequence, dispose of his acres,[36] outside of his tribe, to a Spaniard or to an American.

Before that time there had been encroachment on Indian land. In a letter[37] to Rev. Fray Don Benito Pereyrot, Governor Alberto Maynez wrote on April 19, 1819, ''The league of land of the pueblo of Taos must be counted as 500 varas from the cross

36. Blackmar. Spanish Institutions in the Southwest.
37. Archive—Santa Fe Museum.

of the cemetery to all directions, so that the conflict with the neighbors' land will not be so grave.'' Evidently the conflict went on for the Indian agent, John Greiner, living in Taos in the early fifties wrote, ''The pueblo Indians are planting their grounds, digging their acequias, herding their stock and making every effort to support themselves by their own industry. Could they be protected from the depredations of the Mexican they would not only be examples for their red brethern but for some other people of a lighter complexion.''

In 1852, this same agent referred to the Taos Indians as about five or six hundred in number and added, ''Although they have been much annoyed by the Mexican taking water from their acequias and grazing their stock upon pueblo pasture lands, they have but few complaints to make and appear prosperous, contended and happy.'' This is about as true today as it was seventy-five years ago.

The controversy over water rights would not down. In 1893, the matter came into the courts. This time it was definitely a case between the Taos Indians and the people of Arroyo Seco. In 1818, a ditch was built which headed on Indian land. There was usually plenty of water for all and the Indians did not object but gave permission for the building of the ditch. In times of water shortage, however, they claimed the water, naturally. Such a season was that of the spring of 1893 and, according to testimony taken in court in July, the people of Arroyo Seco had appeared armed at the head of their water supply, ready to fight and demanding all the water

THE PUEBLO OF THE TAOS INDIANS.

Courtesy of H. E. High

they wished. There also came to light the story of preparation for an even greater fight in 1838 and the tale of the surco of water which had been granted the people of Arroyo Seco in 1818. This surco was recorded as the amount of water which could pass through the hub of an old Mexican wheel.

The following court gives us this interesting glimpse of an attempt to replace the old wheel apparently in 1838 and the subsequent trouble.

José Rafael Gallegos a resident of El Prado born in 1813 gave the following testimony in 1893 concerning the quarrel over the amount of water the Arroyo Seco people should have from the pueblo ditch.

"A. When they took the wheel up there to place it, they didn't like it.

Q. And then what did they do?

A. Then the water overseers and the judges were quarreling there with the people from the other place; they couldn't settle; about this time the judges and the water over-seers and the people from the other place began to get mad, and they wanted to decide it by arms, with weapons; they fixed a day on which to encounter each other, and at the head of the faction on this side was Pascual Martinez and the late Miguel Sanchez headed the other faction; the people of the other side took the other side of the dam, and the people from this side, took this side. About this time a thick cloud appeared; the contending officers said that on the first command, they should open fire on both sides. About this time the cloud poured down water, the water was so abundant

that the parties on the north made for a place that
was near by full of willows, and the other parties on
the other side made for a similar place on the south
side.   Within an hour afterwards the water came
down rushing in such an abundance that it went beyond its limits and swept everything before it.   In
that condition of things, neither of them could get
over the river; the northern party went their way
and we went our way.   I was there.''

Q. Were you with the Indians or the people?

A. I was with the Indians, because the people
of this side[38] supported the Indians.''

About three years ago, the Indians and Mexicans decided it was necessary to hold a meeting to
discuss their troubles again, thereby setting a good
example, by the way, for townfolk. After the meeting one of the Indians was asked how the decision
went.

"Oh," he replied, "the Mexicans are to have
one-third and we are to have a third.''

"How about the other third,'' was the natural
query.

"Oh, that's all the water there is in summer,''
came the positive answer.

And so the matter was settled to the satisfaction of all.

*   *   *   *   *   *

Up to about fifty years ago the life of the Taos
Indian in spite of the white man, was much as it had

38. Taos side. Pascual Martinez at the head.

been for centuries as far as his home, his ceremonies and his hunting trips went. Still they called out, "The lightening will give you luck. The thunder will take care of you!" as the hunting parties left for the plains. They carried with them long poles so that the meat might be jerked and dried before they returned. With the hunters went a few young boys for the real work fell on them while the fun and the danger of the hunt was for men. It was, however, harder and harder, to find the buffalo. For years ruthless slaughter of the buffalo and especially the buffalo cow had brought a wealth of robes for the trader and the deadly "fire-water" for the Indians at the forts. Greed and thirst were clearing the plains.

There are still a few Indians living who can tell of buffalo hunts though each year their number is less. The late respected Ventura Romero used to tell of a trip he took into the country near the present Clayton. He was probably about sixteen years old when he was allowed to go along. When once in the haunts of the buffalo, the party made camp. The leader whose word was law—the Mayor Domo—ordered Romero with probably one other to go scouting and to give the regular Indian signal if he found buffalo. Away the boys went and soon they were riding around and around in a short circle. The buffalo were found but as there were only three and there was danger of their escaping, Romero killed them. Up rode the party of older hunters. The Mayor Domo had ordered Romero not to kill and when he found what he had done he was very angry and sent the boy back to camp in disgrace and commanded him to act as cook.

The next day, Romero saw the hunters ride away and sorrowfully took up his camp duties. The long day passed. The hunting party returned tired and unhappy for no buffalo had been seen. There was however good meat sizzling over the fire—meat for all. Romero had shot a lone buffalo which had wandered near the camp.

This luck of the boy set the Mayor Domo to thinking. Finally he sought out Romero and said, "The Great Spirit was displeased with my order. He did not want you punished. You shall go again on the hunt." So it was that Romero gained renown as a buffalo hunter.

The last buffalo hunt of the Taos Indians as a group took place in 1884. Right after the San Geronimo fiesta of that year, forty or fifty left for the east. They were off for the land now called the Pan-handle of Texas. Guns for the most part had displaced the bows and arrows but there were still some who trusted more to a good bow than any white man's shooting stick. The lightening would bring them luck and luck they did have. They found the buffalo but he was grazing peacefully among cattle. Fifty-four were soon killed and the meat jerked. The six tongues which our townsman William L. McClure bought about Christmas time when the hunters returned were the last he ever had a chance to buy. A grand pow-pow was held at the pueblo, described as "mostly noise." The buffalo hunt was over—over forever.

Two years later news came into the pueblo that there were many antelope over in the Cañada del Agua near Tres Piedras and the lower Arroyo Hondo. Again a party started. There was no hunt. It was a "surround" with never a chance for the animal. It was just slaughter. Four hundred antelopes fell among the rocks of their chosen winter home. Never since then have they been seen in any numbers in this country. The antelope hunt too was over —over forever.

Now the Taos Indian give their "buffalo dance," usually early in January. As they sway their nude bodies and long flowing hair they recall the buffalo feeding on the plains. Then stepping more gaily, they lift their arrows as if to hunt again. Old men look far into the past as they drum. They teach in the darkness of the kivas that some day a great earthquake or some catastrophe will cause all white men to disappear from the face of the earth. Then will the red man rule again alone and far across the plains dark herds of buffalo will gladden his eyes and he will be once more on the hunt.

Sometimes this buffalo dance is given on Christmas day[39] and then the chief calls out from the housetops that the deer dance will be given on the sixth of January.

Before this day comes several events occur. A new governor is sworn in by government officials on the first of January. He has previously been chosen by the council of the old men of the pueblo.

39. The Christmas celebration at the pueblo is most unique. I have described this in "Taos Today" 'and so omit it here.

The cacique or priest names several men for this honor and then one is elected. When once his oath is given, men bring into his house the strong box in which are the precious documents and archives of days gone by. With this is brought a bundle of old-time crosses and the new chief is handed his insignia of authority—the cane sent by Abraham Lincoln to the Taos pueblo as a token of his gratitude for the loyalty of the Taos Indians to the Union.

This cane is not the only one in use. For many years another cane or staff has been in the hands of governors. When a man is summoned before the council, this old cane is taken to the door of his home. This he recognizes as an order for him to appear before the old men to answer to some charge. When he is sworn to tell the truth, he places his hand on the cane and not on the Bible.

Here it seems in place to say that there are not many cases which are brought before the council The Indian respects the laws of the pueblo, as a rule, and these are all that are necessary in their life. This was evidently the belief of Judge Watts who wrote the following opinion in 1869 and most people who know the Indian of today will second these statements. Judge Watts wrote:

"This court has known the conduct and habits of these Indians (the Pueblos) for eighteen or twenty years, and we say, without the fear of successful contradiction, that you may pick out one thousand of the best Americans in New Mexico, and one thousand of the best Mexicans in New Mexico, and one thousand of the worst pueblo Indians, and there will be found less, vastly less, murder, robbery, theft, or other crimes among the thousand of the worst pueblo Indians than among the thousand of the best Mexicans or Americans in New Mexico. The associate justice now beside me, Hon. Joab Houghton has been judge and lawyer in this territory for over twenty years, and the chief justice for seventeen years, and during all that time not twenty pueblo Indians have been brought before the courts in all New Mexico, accused of violation of the criminal laws of this territory.''[40]

Sometimes the governor is against the white man and tries to keep all Indians from posing for the artists or making any unnecessary trips into town. He calls the Indians about him on Sundays often and speaks after this manner, ''God made us Indians and He wants us to be always Indians. Hold to your Indian beliefs, your Indian customs. Keep all in your heart and you will live long time but if you tell to white man you will die.'' One shrewd governor said some years ago, ''It becomes us to act ignorant and foolish, like children and that way we get more protection from the government.''

There is now and then a governor who has an aggressive spirit and more of an understanding of the white man's friendship. He orders the roads repaired. A summon is made from the house-top as usual, about the first of April. All the men respond to this call or are forced to pay a fine. Some years

40. Case—United States v. Lucero. Sup. Ct. Jan. 1869—Opinion of the Court—C. J. Watts. P. 441-2 New Mexico Reports Vol. I.
    In November, 1925, an Indian stabbed another to death. This is said to be the only murder committed at the pueblo in fifty years.

ago the repairing of the road but, especially the opening up of the ditches for irrigation purposes, was begun by an old ceremony including a prayer for their fields. This does not take place now but, at the close of the work, the chief thanks the men for heeding his request for laborers. This appreciation keeps the Indians loyal.

Once in a while, a governor reverts to old-time punishments after a meeting with the council of wise men in an estufa. In 1923, an order was given to confine some offender in the stocks. This was too much for the younger Indians who brought the news to town, not only of this but of very heavy and unjust fines. This resulted in the retirement of the governor.

It was not long ago that their belief in witchcraft led to one man being accused and condemned to die. Relatives begged for his life which was finally spared and the man fined. Later, when talking of this belief he was heard to say, "How can I believe in that. They accused *me* of being a wizard." For once the "other fellow" spoke. This belief in witches shows itself, now and then, when some one accuses another of having "witched" some afflicted person. They also believe they can wish injury to any one who comes to the pueblo and proves to be unwelcome.

In the minds of the young at this Indian community there is growing up a strong belief that if their governor proves unfair to them they may appeal for justice from the United States government for which they have a profound respect in spite of the fact that it has done little for this particular

WAR DANCE OF THE WOMEN

Awa Tsireh

group of wards. Only a few weeks ago two Indian boys were whipped for insisting on wearing American clothes. This means they discarded the leggings or half trousers and blanket for the usual dress of an American boy. Some boys also refusing to let their hair grow long to be worn in two plaits on the shoulders as is the wont of the older men. The boys who got in trouble reported the matter and the case goes to the U. S. court this spring.

Again about two or three years ago when a young man came back from the army he was threatened with a ducking if he would not dance. The Chiffonettes pulled him into the midst of the dancers but still Tony refused to take the old-time steps. Again came a threat of a forced bath in a cold January river but the older Indians did not care to do other than threaten. The father of the boy who, some twenty years ago, is said to have been one of those who did most to make it uncomfortable, to say the least, for the soldier who returned from the ranks in 1898, came out very positively with the statement, "They have no right to treat my boy so. He wears soldiers clothes." Back of the son he knew stands "the Great Father' 'in Washington.

Even the Indian woman knows that she may appeal for justice to the council of the old men. About six years ago, a woman appeared before them and complained that an Indian had followed her into the woods near the stream where she, with others, were washing clothes. He attempted to carry her away with him according to the story all told. He was hailed before the court and his fine was that he

surrender to the woman three-fourths of his prop-
erty. What American jury would have done as well?

So much for the older people, now let us look at
the children on the third of January. Boys, from ten
to thirteen years of age, go away in single file to
the mountains. They seek out a clay pit, they know
of, and fill their bags of old cloth with a goodly load,
swing it on their backs and return ki-hi-ing as they
walk. When once at the river, they cease singing.
A group of boys forms on either side of the narrow
stretch of ice. They busy themselves making small
balls of clay which they put on an end of a stick and
then the "mud battle" begins. Behind each group
stand their elders urging them on, telling them of
brave ancestors and how they used to fight. They
pelt each other until one side is forced to retire.
Then they pick up sticks and engage in a close fight,
striking savage blows at their opponents until again
the stronger side wins. When once this happens the
boys who win are patted on the back and taken to a
feast given by losers. Their lesson in personal brav-
ery is over for the time.

When the ice has begun to break along this same
stream the boys gather and loop up supple willow
branches with horse hair and learn to catch fish
Indian fashion. Sometimes on the old log bridge a
few will try again the battle of the sticks and many
a hapless one gets a ducking if he loses his balance.
Again in the sunshine of spring days, a group of
boys toss a knife—a game very old and played by
the Chinese children across the big western water.

By the time January sixth has arrived all is in

readiness for the big dance—the deer dance. The beating of a drum in the kivas announces that the dancers are coming. Then up the ladders they come nude save for the bright colored breech-clout and covered with deer skins. They bend over as they walk with short sticks in their hands which reach the ground.

Two queens lead the procession of men and most serious and dignified are they throughout the dance. They are usually dressed in white buckskin with gay ribbons for color and in their hands they carry small branches of pine. They represent all that is best in animal as well as human life. Following them come two men with huge deer horns painted white and these lead the men now in parallel lines and then about in a circle, in front of the church.

When the serious side of the ceremony is over, the Chiffonettes come into the group and with faces quite hideous with black and white markings they caper about with bows from which they shoot straw arrows. Then seizing some small boy from the dancers, one of these clowns playfully tries to make his get-away through the group of bystanders. An Indian who represents the protecting spirit makes after the young boy deer to rescue him. In this dance as in the buffalo dance there are always, on the side, men who represent an invisible god spirit who guards the buffalo or the deer.

As is the custom, when the dance is over in one place the whole group of people move to another place along that race course on the south side of the northern pueblo. Then again, bending over, the men become the deer and solemnly repeat the steps of the dance which is really a ceremony, a prayer for power to hunt the deer. Indeed, long, long ago when the deer spoke the same language, he told the Indians how to have this ceremony in order to have power over him and get their flesh for food and their skins for dress. So it is necessary for them to practice many times before they give the dance in the open. Years ago they would not let any unbelievers see the ceremony because that would render it less effective. They do not object today. They are not so dependant upon the deer of the mountains, as in the days of old.

I have also been told that the deer dance is given in grateful remembrance of a time when the whole pueblo were in dire need of food, in danger of famine, in fact. While wandering up on the mountainside, a party of Indian women came on deer sign and hurried to the pueblo and summoned the hunters who soon had enough for all and the Taos tribe was saved. Whether this be a true story back of this dance I do not know but I do know that these deer Indians are most picturesque. I do not wonder that a Taos hurriedly returned from New York City this winter because he explained, "The deer dance is the greatest thing in the world. There is nothing else like it."

The month of January ends with an inspection of arms. This comes early in the morning of the thirtieth and the Indian men paint themselves and make a gala day of the affair, sometimes dancing a goodly part of the day.

During the following month there comes a series of dances which are really given as a sort of encouragement to the boys who are to go into retirement for religious education. Some times it is a Navajo dance with its circle of drummers and singers on the ground. A broken circle of women with hands outstretched make their way about the men in the center while a larger outer circle of young Indians slowly march around. Sometimes it is the Apache gift dance, when two sets of singers and drummers sit on either side of a space where a couple beautifully dressed dance. The man takes the more violent steps; the woman moves very gently over the ground making progress by inches only.

Then for forty days the older Indians do ''work for the sun'' choosing a different kiva or estufa each year. During this time the old men sit in a circle, eat only corn food and wild game and initiate the boys of nine to fourteen years. Then is the time that the old stories are told, of how the Taos Indians came out of that lake near the Sierra Blanca, of how they received from God—perhaps Montezuma—the corn and pumpkin seed which made them pueblos while deer horns and hair made the plains Indians. They learn that the Earth is their Mother and the Sun the great Father. ''The Sun travels every day and it never gets tired and we should do likewise,'' is a bit of advice given. ''The work for the Sun'' probably consists in many prayers and the Taos Indians believe the white man should be grateful to them because it is this ''work'' which makes the Sun willing to shine on the earth.

Not long ago the coming total eclipse of the sun was much talked of. The section of country over which this would be clearly visible was not definitely known by some of our townspeople. They told the Indians about what was to happen but though they listened they were very doubtful about the matter. When the day came, some in town as well as at the pueblo were on top of the houses looking toward the east. Taos was too far west to catch even a glimpse of the eclipse. The sun came to us as usual. It was not long before Indians appeared in town to say "You see the white man does not know everything."

On another occasion an artist explained at great length about a partial eclipse which was to come. Dark smoked glasses were in readiness. The Indians came as usual to work about the place. Some time later, to their astonishment the Indian saw the face of the sun begin to darken. They refused to look through the glasses. They dropped their tools where they were and hurried to the pueblo where for four days they prayed for the Sun. The white man's word meant nothing. It was only too evident to them that the "Sun was sick." The "Fon-si-ni" or Americans do not know everything!

Here, in the estufas the old men teach the boys the history of their tribe and show them how they must continue to "work for the Sun." They tell them of the mysteries of life as well as the secrets of their people which none but Indians must ever know. As far as I know none but the Indians do know either to this day.[41]

---

41. Of these, one Indian said, "They are mostly foolishess."

After the first forty days, a smaller group of boys are chosen from those first selected.[42] Not all boys go on with the religious education as it is called. The chosen ones then go to a room on top or near the top of the pueblo where women wearing black and yellow leggings attend to their wants. Young men play their part in the ceremonies. They wear yellow trousers cut with a wide flap at the bottom and struck across with hand marks of red paint. These colors all have their meaning,—but let the Indian tell.

Later the boys go to the cañon for a month where they "make medicine" a ceremony for the testing out of strength and daring apparently. The training of body, mind and especially memory continues for about a year and a half. On August 6th of the following year the boys may again go home, to be known thereafter by a new name. When once in the school room again, teachers testify to the value of their Indian training for minds are more quick, more alert and memories notably improved.

Again and again when some of the more promising boys are called away from school[43] to spend this

42. This spring, one family refused to allow a boy to take this religious education after he was chosen by the council. As far as known, this is the first case on record.

43. The government has been most remiss in the matter of education for the Indian. It is only about twenty-five years ago that the first girls were sent to Santa Fe to school. Often only one boy in a family was allowed by the Indians to go for they did not want to part with their little children any more than the white men do. Finally a school was established here but for years no effort was made to give instruction beyond the third grade. Two years ago a building was made to accomodate higher grades. The buildings were constructed after plans made back east with a ruler and by minds sadly inelastic. The pueblo offered something beautiful in plan. "Could not something be done in the way of appealing to Washington to build something in harmony with surroundings," i asked. No, such a hope could not be entertained. So up went the ugly buildings and the nearby home for teachers, made to conform to a T square but foreign to any idea of home or comfort.

year and a half the government has tried to have
some arrangement made whereby the boys will not
have to lose this time in school. As yet, however,
the Indians have not seen the wisdom of making a
change in their old custom so as to be more fair to
the growing boy. This will come in time of course.
No one asks the Indians to give up this training but
do ask that the time be better divided. "It is too
bad that your boy has to be out of school," said a
teacher to an Indian father who sees farther into the
future than most. His reply connotes much, "I am
sorry too but, you see, I am bound by the rules of
this pueblo."

Meantime while the boys are away from their
homes, life goes on in the pueblo as it has for so long.
In the seven estufas, various clans hold their meet-
ings at different times. Of these societies, we may
give the names of some. There are the Corn people
—and those of the Sun, Rain, Big House-makers—
Big-earing, Root, Water, Fire, Shell, Black-eyed or
Chiffonettes, and others. Two or three clans use one
kiva as their meeting place.

All of these clans have the same beliefs however. They still have in practically every home fet-
ishes. These are small stone images of animals. I
recently held one. It was an image of a bear made
of black stone which had "come down from the an-
cients." It fit the hand and that is where the Indian
likes to hold it for it gives him courage and strength
in a fight.

Around the neck of many a man hangs his bag

THE GREEN CORN CEREMONY

Awa Tsireh

of charms.[44] These vary of course. Some have an old arrow or an elk's tooth, or a bit of powdered wood from a tree which has been struck by lightning. This is considered especially "good medicine" to have. Then there is a small claw and many another little things which will go in the bag. These are worn especially while on the hunt for they believe these charms will keep them invisible to the guardian spirit of the deer and buffalo who is also invisible as has been said. This gives them the belief that they will be successful in their hunt, so on they go.

Among the stories of the Indian hunters, there are several good tales of encounters with bears. The noted hunter of today is called Mirabal or "Geronimo, the bear hunter." The following are well-known true stories.

Sometime during the late eighties, four or five men took the trails over the mountains to Moreno Valley and beyond. They made their brush camp and then gun in hand followed bear signs. One of the men was soon close upon his animal, lifted his gun and fired. The bear was wounded but kept on his way, the hunter after him. Suddenly Mr. Bruin decided to call this man's "bluff." Turning sharply he made for him. There was no time to use the gun

---

44. This wearing of charms is not limited to the Indians. Most children of Mexican descent wear such today. Not long ago, it rained just after plans for a picnic had been discussed in a school room. The teacher was sympathizing with the little folk when Marie walked quietly to her desk and whispered, "I can stop the rain." She went to the window and took out a hidden charm, a small picture of a saint. Her lips moved in fervent prayer. In a few minutes it happened that the rain abated. There were smiles for the moment. Then it began to rain harder than ever. Again Marie declared she could stop the rain if she only had some salt. "Salt?" asked the teacher. "Why salt?" "I would throw it this way and that," asid the little girl making the sign of the cross. It continued to rain. Marie had no salt.

again so the man struck a heavy brow. This hardly
bothered the animal who promptly took the gun and
threw it many yards away. Then came the hand to
hand struggle with the bear naturally getting the
best of it, gnawing the muscles of first one arm then
the other. Finally the struggle was too much for man
and beast. They both fell to the ground. The man
was fast for one arm was under the bear. He could
not pull away and the bear was too nearly gone to
continue the punishment of his Indian. Lying there
on the ground together the Indian began talking to
the bear, "I didn't kill you. You'd better not kill
me." The days when animals and Indians understood each other seemed to have come back. Over and
over again, the Indian argued with the dying bear, "I
didn't kill you. You had better not kill me," pushing
back the bear's face the while with his free arm. It
just seemed to me he understood," said the Indian
later.

Death had however its firm grip on the bear and
soon he rolled over, rose and shambled slowly away.
The Indian too rose and painfully made his way back
to the camp. Here of course he found aid. Later he
was put on his horse and the whole party made for
the pueblo. It was long weary months before the
young Taos Indian was able to forget for a moment
that bear enemy of his.

Juan Romero is another bear hunter who went
over into the Rio Grande country. He met his bear
too, accompanied by two cubs. "He had a good gun.
He had a Winchester. He had no time to load it.
The bear slapped him," said an Indian in telling me

the story. Evidently the bear slapped well for soon
Romero was flat on the ground playing his last trick
for life. The bear slapped again, played with the
man's body as a cat would with a mouse. Romero
never moved a muscle. He was playing dead. So
well did he make good his part that the bear was
fooled and left for her journey on over the rocks. Her
victim lived many a long year to tell the tale.

"After church," said Lake Talk when telling
his bear story, "I went up on the big rocky mountain and over on the other side. There was a nice
good spring of pure water. There were flowers,
yellow and purple all around and butterflies flying
around me. I was resting. My gun—I was holding
by my side here. Soon I heard a noise back of me.
And I saw a bear. It was comin' down the brooks—
look for the ant. Before he saw me, I saw him. Before he knew, I shoot him. My little yellow dog hold
him in the neck and I shoot him in the head again.
Then I skin him. I hang it up in a big wood. I took
a piece of meat and bring it home. The next morning I went after him on horseback. When I get up,
then I put him on horseback and I bring him home.
When I bring it home, the old man put up a wire and
hung the meat to dry."

So go the bear stories but not all Indians aspire
to being able to tell such stories. In fact, there are
but few who really seek the bears. More often than
not, one gets this, which came from as brave an Indian as there is at the pueblo. "I tell you. When I
come on bear track, I jes leave it alone. It can go

on," said he, with a generous wave of the arm. "*I follow deer track.*"

When hunting parties come in from the mountains there is almost sure to be some young fellow who has a deerskin to dress. When the skin is very white he makes a pair of woman's boots—his present to his bride.

He met his girl at the school probably and shyly talked with her. He danced with her at the school parties and now though both are still in their teens he proposes marriage.[45] Everything is confided to the parents and then plans are underway for an engagement party. This takes place at the home of the bride-to-be. All of her people gather first and then, in a body, come those of the groom. They sit around on the floor and ask questions and consider the proposed marriage from every angle.

One man has charge of the ceremony. The young couple kneel. The boy is asked first if he wishes the marriage. One fellow dared to say, not long ago, "It ought to be ladies first, no?" Then the girl is asked if she consents to being married. One recently was asked what she would answer, "Oh, I'll say yes, if he does," came the quick reply. When the two have answered in Spanish, upon being asked their names, the master of ceremonies takes from each a rosary and presents it to the other. Then a prayer is offered in Spanish. The two are engaged.

When the service is over, the two go out into

---

45. Not long ago, a shy young bridegroom came to the plaza for a license. He knew of but one place to go. He asked for a license in few words and it was promptly made out. On handing it to the priest, he learned he had procured a license to fish!

THE RACES ON SAN GERONIMO DAY
Photograph of 1886.

Courtesy of W. L. McClure

another room to eat with their relatives but the couple are never together. They do not even speak to each other. After eating of a great variety of food, they all go in to see the presents. A new trunk from the bridegroom's home is opened. There are dresses and material for more, soap, dishes, jewelry, beads, pins, belts and the *boots,* for no matter what the season, the groom has "got his deer' and there are new white buck-skin boots for his bride.

Two weeks after the two are married usually in the church in town. The first use of the wedding ring was in December, 1922, when Rufina Romero and Joe Archuleta were married. On the day of the ceremony there is a feast but no presents are made. Then the couple go to the home of the bride where they live for a while. Later they go to their own little home. As a rule these marriages are fairly happy but there are good men and women in the pueblo and bad as well. There are those who claim to be aristocrats and others who make no such claim. There are good husbands and others are cruel. The story is much the same when one writes of the white man. It is true, however, that white men would not live in as much harmony were they living in such close quarters to their neighbors as have these Indians for so many generations. The old men mean that marriages shall be happy. One young buck who went without his bride to the pueblo school parties and became known soon as a flirt was recently sent home by order of the council and told that he could no longer go to the dances.

*   *   *   *   *   *

Spring days are courting days the world over, so, too, are they planting days. No matter what the government farmer may say in the way of advice, it is not until the chief calls out from the house-tops that the morrow is the appointed day for planting, that the Indian farmer makes a move. Preceding this in March, there is a ceremony in the fields when prayers are offered and a good ear of corn, carefully laid in an ornamented buck-skin bag filled with soft eagle's down, is buried in the ground with the proper appeal to the Sun to grant a good crop.

During the early summer come the ''corn dances'' in which the men and women in gay dress dance for the Sun. Each dance forms one of a series which are prayers for the seed, the germination, the growth, and the ripening of the corn. They are prayers to their God to grant them a goodly harvest. When this comes they give their San Geronimo fiesta, so named by the friars who long ago persuaded the Indians to advance the day they had celebrated for centuries, probably, to co-incide with the saint's day.

On the evening of the twenty-ninth comes the ''Sun-down Dance'' when men with branches, green and yellow, signifying the full run of the season, dance out of the church yard and about the pueblo. It is the culminating ceremony—their prayer of gratitude to their visible God—the Sun. They worship in the pueblo chapel, as do white men. The God of the chapel is in reality the God of their fields. The Indian chooses to worship in the great out-doors and in the way he best understands.

During the closing days of August, the Indians
have a different type of dance far up in the mountains to which no white man dare go. They have a
right to exclude all and they do so. This dance is,
however, understood by the white man by what Indians themselves have intimated. It is the one dance
to which the so-called reformers have a right to object, in the name of fair play for the Indian woman.
Girls and childless women are forced to go to the
mountain. So thoroughly is this against the wish of
the Indian women, though long used to the custom,
that daughters of the pueblo, now and then, prefer
exile to returning from the government schools and
having to submit to this ceremony imposed upon
them by the older men. Younger men have been
known to admit quite frankly that this summer dance
by the lake is unfair to the girls. Those who have
ventured far in the white man's world have come
back with word that it is high time to abolish the
custom.[46] A man who knows Indians well recently
said with a sorry shake of the head, ''I have seen the
girls come back looking like wilted flowers.''

The day will come when the young girls who now
are in the majority in the higher classes at the government school, which, since 1924 only, carries the
Indian children beyond the third grade—these girls
whose eyes shine bright with an awakening mind,
some of whom are chosen to go through with certain

---

46. My authorities for what I have said in this paragraph are of the
best. I will add this—a prominent Indian recently read an article
on the subject of this particular custom. When finished he re-
marked, ''That fellow knows what he is talking about,'' and later
added, something to the effect that he guessed it would have to
go. This is the opinion which is certainly growing among the
Indians. They are well able to manage the matter themselves
and will do so before long without doubt.

tribal training each spring,—*these girls* will demand
justice. The boy of today will be the man of the
morrow and I have faith to believe that he is the coming champion for the girls of his tribe. It is only as
it comes from within the tribe itself that any real
change can be effected. The white man should keep
his hands off and cease his prattle.

Neither is the white man needed in the present
quarrel at the pueblo over the use of peyote. At present it is said about fifteen percent of the Indians
are peyote users. This is not the place for a lengthy
discussion concerning the use of this cactus root
which blossoms white only about an inch above the
ground in northern Mexico. The button-like hard
flower is eaten raw, stewed and sometimes ground
very fine and put in capsules. It evidently does not
affect all in the same way but usually it acts like a
drug, producing visions or at least feelings of joy
and benevolence toward all. Its use is made the
center of religious ceremonies and this has sometimes been referred to as but a cloak to hide a drug
habit. Those who are users declare it is most bene-
ficial while those who are against it state as positively that it is most harmful and results in the complete
demoralization of the character of the user while
producing a physical state of lassitude not conducive
to honest labor.

As far back as 1569 we have Bernardino Saha-
gun writing in old Mexico against the 'evil mush-
rooms which intoxicate like wine,'' and, in the twen-
ties of our century, men like Dr. E. L. Hewitt declaring that he does not believe the peyote harmful

Courtesy of Francis Riche

CHIFFONETTIS CLIMBING THE POLE.
Their aim is to secure to prize sheep and food to be used in the San Geronimo evening feast—1925.

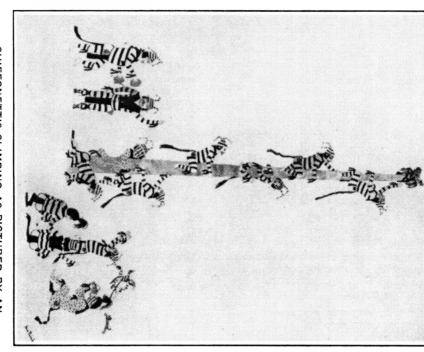

CHIFFONETTIS CLIMBING AS PICTURED BY AN INDIAN ARTIST.

while another stated, "It is about as harmful as coffee." We find the old padres declaring against its use, writing, "It is almost as grave a sin as eating human flesh" and the present day priest unwilling to take any definite side of the question. One really need take no side. The Indian will find out to his satisfaction and settle the matter, in time.

It is interesting to read in the old archive about the trial held at the pueblo in the early spring of 1720. It seems some boys made a great racket "down by the cottonwoods" and when hailed before a court declared the herb had been given them by an interpreter who had come in from the Moquis. He had evidently told an old man who had lost something that the boys who ate the herb would help him find his treasure. Apparently it did not work that way but did set the boys to having a jubilee which was not to the liking of the rest of the pueblo folk. Finally the offending visitor from the Moquis was sentenced to be lashed. As the people had requested that "for God's sake, he be sent from the pueblo," he evidently left in a hurry.[47]

This spring a similar affair took place only a few weeks ago. Boys who use peyote made the night uncomfortable with their noise. When arrested they declared they were making the noise because it was part of their religion. Then the charge was made to read, "For disturbing the peace." The two factions evidently had had a hand to hand fight if scratches tell tales for when the boys refused to pay their fines

---

47. Archive in Santa Fe Museum. 1719-1720. Translation by Rev. Lansing Bloom.

the other side tried to take their blankets away from them. This resulted of course, in a tussle.

The more one learns of the ceremonies of the peyote users and the effects which it seems to have on the modern Indian, the less one is inclined to be of the opinion that the revival of the old use of the drug is in anyway a step in advance in Indian life. The problem is, however, one the Indian himself must work out at present at least. The time came when the habit of drinking liquor became a curse to Indian and white man and the government finally took a hand in the matter. So it will do again if peyote makes it necessary.

Now we return to the end of the season of the dances. When the San Geronimo fiesta[48] is passed there come busy days under temporary tents when corn husking goes on at the bidding of the chief. Wood is brought in from the mountains and piled in stacks. Meat is hung on long lines to dry, for winter days are coming. After a few weeks, the thought of the spring months begins again to dominate the Indian's mind.

December sixth finds the Indians putting up their wagons. They mount their horses and ride to town. No wagon comes over the road from the pueblo unless it be driven by some Indian revolutionist, as we may term him. "It is a custom of the old men" will be the explanation made. It is in reality a season sacred to the Sun when as little noise as possible

48. There is a similar day of racing and feasting on May third. These races from east to west again link up with the Sun worship— races which will bring the Sun across its old path in the Heavens so that the Indian may have good crops. In the afternoon comes the Corn Dance, signifying the planting of the corn.

is to be made in the pueblo. Women do not sew—at least on the white man's machine, nor do they cut their hair which they usually wear in bangs that cover the eyebrows. Girls grind no corn nor do boys sing or put on any paint. The time belongs to their own religion. There are but three days of any gaiety, December 25th, January 1st and January 6th.

During this period of about five weeks, certain societies are appointed to go a *Pa-si-tah* or open space just beyond Glorieta in the cañon. Here they pray for an early summer and good crops. As they sit around in a circle, a medicine man stands among them and offers the spoken prayer. They have plenty of food with them and stay all day, "making medicine in the woods." When once this season of prayer is over the day comes again when the Indians may use their wagons. Very early on that morning the pueblo is awakened with much ki-hi-ing and a great ado is made. There is much joy on this day when the rattle of wagons may again be heard down the roads.

There have been some sad days during the fall and winter and it is small wonder that there is great rejoicing on that early January day. Behind them lies All Souls Day, November 2nd, when in a long solemn procesion of men and women have visited the graves of their loved ones, where they leave food as do the Chinese in the far-away orient. When the twilight hour comes a smaller group of silent folk go up the cañon just beyond the old wall to the east and here in little secluded places are left bottles of milk and the like for the little ones who died before they could gladden the hearts of their parents.

*　　*　　*　　*　　*　　*

During long winter evenings the fathers of the pueblo have told their children stories of their ancestors. "Once upon a time" begins well this story of the great destruction of all the Indians. Only the old chief was left. He fashioned out of clay, first, a coyote and on this he breathed. Then he molded a bird and it flew in the air. Finally he modeled a woman and another man. He breathed on them and lo, they too lived! So there came upon the earth again the Indians.

Then, too, away up in the mountains is a beautiful lake—Blue Lake. From that depression long ago came the deer and the buffalo. Then the white man came and had a bad influence. The lake filled with water and that is why there are so few animals now in the mountains.

There is the eagle—the sacred bird. He could talk once to the Indians. In fact, his feathers make good "eagle medicine" and bring speed to runners. Below him close to the earth is the rattlesnake. He can still talk. Why, not long ago, an artist in town was bitten by a rattlesnake. Before he had rid himself of the painful poison, an Indian friend came to see him and told him he knew he was going to be bitten. One day, while he was in the woods, he heard voices, telling how this man was to be stung because some one had wished him ill luck. Looking about to

Courtesy of ART AND ARCHAEOLOGY, Washington, D. C.

LOS MATACHINES

Awa Tsireh

see who was talking, the Indian could not discover a soul. Examining the ground nearby, he found two rattlesnakes—snakes which had been talking!

Yes, there are brujos.[49] There is a Devil too. The Indian is sure of that. Quills of centuries ago wrote of this devil.

Peter Martyr, a learned Protestant divine wrote his "Decades of the Newe Worlde" about 1550. In this he told "of the familiaritie which certeyne of the Indians have with the devyll and howe they receave answere of him of thygnes to coome," and adds seriously, "the devyell beynge so auncient an Astronomer knoweth the tymes of thynges and seeth howe they are naturally directed." Later in 1721, Father Charlevois wrote of several things which he had seen while among the Indians and declared these seemed proof to him "that the Devil is sometimes concerned in the magic of the Savages."

Not long ago a Taos assured me that the brujos or brujas, which correspond to the wizards and witches of the Anglo-Saxons, could kill or disfigure at will. He said the Indians knew of hypnotism long before the white man talked of it. These brujos could not only hypnotize but could come through locked doors, eat and steal but if their identity was

49. There is an old deserted group of houses sometimes called "Buena Vista" on a mesa some five or six miles west of Taos. According to the natives this is the headquarters of the brujos or ghosts. Here, too, live the "little people." These special brujos of Taos were given to swinging out of chimneys in flame and going to the next chimney through the air. There is also that big brujo—"a great big white thing" that comes up out of the Rio Grande Cañon—an excellent place for him to live, by the way. He makes his way along the roads. Then of course there are the brujos who haunt the burying ground of the Indians just out of town to the north. The "tumble weed," light in an autumn wind, gives more than one person a scare as it lifts, falls and makes its way up hill and down dale.

discovered they were doomed to die. This last re-
mark linked these intruders with the living but he
did not seem to notice that. These evil workers went
by the name of "Yea-pa-na" or sleep makers.

Only last spring one of the old men of the pueblo
awakened all the old-time beliefs by declaring that
he had seen a bruja, a woman nude save for a gray
rag fluttering about her, as her long hair floated to
the wind. On that March evening, this bruja ventured forth from the old church along the path to the
new chapel. Where she went and on what errand she
was bent no one knew but for a while the whole pueblo was deeply stirred and many were the tales told
in hushed breath behind the adobe walls of Indian
homes.

Among these was probably the story of a lover
of some eighty years ago. He seems to have guessed
that his sweetheart had the power to hypnotize, or
was at least one of the brujas then appearing.

One night he saw a light in his sweetheart's
home. He approached cautiously and pushed back the
rag which was stuffed in the small hole of a window.
Then he could see his beloved and her two sisters
dancing in witch attire as the old mother sang and
patted her knee beating time. He overheard her tell
the girls to go to the three bridges which then
spanned the river.

Hiding in a corn crib at the foot of the ladder,
the lover waited, holding in his teeth a flint and one
in his hand so that he need not come under the hyp-
notic spell of his girl. He watched her come down the
ladder and then boldly caught her by the wrist be-

fore she could rush away to that center bridge to which she had been told to go.

Noting her dress of a bit of cloth and long free hair, he reproached her angrily, "You ought to be ashamed. You have got to go to the bridge and get cleaned up." Once at the river, he threw her into the water and hit her with a willow switch. Then he told her to go home and behave. The words that ended the tale could be no other than, "and in four days she died."

Then too, it was a brujo, an invisible brujo, who helped the young artist twenty-five years ago who came out to the pueblo to race with their swiftest runners. Somehow he was allowed to win, not once but every time. Again a brujo was in that jar the same artist insisted on buying. The Indians told him the jar could not be brought safely to town. It had belonged to the ancestors and should not leave the pueblo but if it did a brujo would surely attend to it. The artist, however, did not listen. He bought the pot, carried it safely in his hand until his boy decided to stop for a bath in a nearby stream. While the lad went for his plunge, the father put the precious jar under the clothes of the boy. For a few minutes he turned to study some passing mood of nature and his mind was with his brushes. The boy, done with his swim, hurried to dress and alas! sat down on his clothes. There was a sharp crack. The jar was broken. At once all the pieces were picked up. When the pot was carefully put together by the disappointed artist, he found one three-cornered piece missing. Through that hole the brujo had escaped. When the story had to be told to the one-time owner of the piece of pottery, he said nothing but turned away with a move that meant, ''I knew you could not get that jar into town.''

There is a brujo no doubt in those boxes in town from which voices and music come. One Indian asked if there was not a little man inside? Another listened to a simple explanation of a radio, heard the music, looked the machine all over. ''Yes, I understand,'' he said, ''but there is just one thing I do not understand. What is it makes it talk?'' You, who do not believe in spirits, explain again.

Once when coming through a cañon an Indian father and son came upon hostile Indians. They stopped among the sage and rabbit-brush. They became coyotes for a time and then when the danger was passed, lo, they were Indians.

Again comes the oft-told story of the giant or *Gigante* who used to live in the valley and when tired would sit on that flat-topped mountain one can easily see, blue on the western horizon. When he was hungry he took one or two steps, grabbed up an Indian and ate him. He left one or two foot-prints up near Red River and there is one to be seen in Taos cañon by the water. In the Indian mind there is no doubt about this. Finally the Spaniards came and they tried to kill him with guns but could not. No! The Indians killed him with bow and arrow. They know—because he does not come any more! Furthermore, the giant bled to death for, far up in the mountains, is a great mound of very red earth. Here the

THE PET EAGLE
Photograph of 1886.

Courtesy of W. L. McClure

Indians go to get the paint for their faces. Apaches secure a fresh supply whenever they come a-visiting.

Some years ago, a friend of mine[50] sat by the road leading to the pueblo, making some notes. An old Indian approached and, hoping for a sale, showed her a bracelet on which was a thunder-bird design.

"No," was her answer. "That design is not correct. It should be so and so."

"How do you know that," said the astonished Indian who leaned over and shook her gently by the shoulder.

"I know about the thunder-bird. Sit down and let me tell you the story," she said. "Years ago the Ojibways told me."

The Indian was soon lost in the tale. He listened with great interest and insisted on corrections for he too knew the legend, the Taos version of it.

It seems that long ago there was a young Indian who had a beautiful eagle. He fed it and cared for it tenderly. So fond did he grow that he would not leave his pet even to do his allotted work. The old men of the pueblo remonstrated with him to no avail. He would not leave the eagle. Finally, since there seemed to be no other way the wise men declared that they would kill the winged favorite unless the young fellow would attend to his work. This threat was too much, and led to a long talk with the eagle. The bird said nothing but fluttered with its wings.

Believing that his pet would really be killed the young man sorrowfully untied the restraining rope

50. Prof. Bessie E. Edsall. The writer has also told this story to a Taos who nodded approval to this version of the story.

and bid his pet fly, fly to safety. The great wings
spread and lifted the eagle far above his head but
it did not fly away. It hovered near and finally was
just above the young man.

"You were kind to me when you thought me but
an eagle. Now I will save you," said the bird comforting the young man who before he knew what was
happening felt himself grasped in the talons of his
pet who soared higher and higher through the blue,
up, up to the hole in the sky, that every good Indian
knows about but can not tell just where it is.

When once beyond all human sight and well
through the hole in the sky, the young man found
himself in the land of the thunder-birds. His eagle
let its feathered dress fall and there stood in gorg-
eous array a beautiful princess. It was her turn to
woo and her bridegroom the young Indian became.
Then they were very happy.

One day the young lover tried on the eagle dress
which had been made for him by his bride so that
he too could fly at will. Then there came over him
the great curiosity so common to humans. He
wandered to the edge of the hole in the sky. He had
been warned never to pass through but his eagle
wings were strong. He would go. All went well.
His wide-spread feathers carried him safely through
into the lower blue.

Enjoying this forbidden pleasure he circled and
circled until suddenly he saw below him the pueblo
of the people who never were and never will be.
Nearer and nearer he drew until he beheld a charming girl with shining eyes and outstretched arms.

He must go to her and for the time all thought of the beautiful land beyond the hole in the sky was forgotten.

The girl of the far away blue had not forgotten. She knew that her eagle bridegroom was gone. She wandered to the hole and looking over saw him far below among the people who never were and never will be. She saw him with the girl of the shining eyes—evil eyes. Quickly she donned her feathered gown and swiftly she cut the air until she again hovered over her beloved. She gathered him in her talons once more and circled and circled through the heavens and was lost to sight through the hole in the sky.

Then came a reconciliation for the beautiful princess loved her human groom and he was again content to live on with her.

Wandering too near the hole one day, the longing to be on the wing overcame him and once more he slipped through on his strong wings and hurried away happy to be free and again he sought out the girl of the shining eyes.

Angry at being deserted for the second time, the princess of the land in the air donned her eagle dress and glided away. She saw her wayward one far below among the people who never were and never will be. Swiftly she flew to him and swooping down caught him up and carried him back, back through the hole in the sky. This time she did not forgive. She told him she despised him. All the thunderbirds no longer loved him. He must go and never return. She tore his eagle dress from him. Then she pushed him to the edge and over into the blue.

Down, down fell the Indian. No wings made his flight smooth and safe. Down, down like a heavy stone he fell through the vast space down to his people. They saw him falling and hastened to the rocks where he soon lay. He was lifeless. His tongue could not tell them of his visit to the people who never were and who never will be nor of the beauty of that land far away beyond the hole in the sky.

While we are listening to Indian tales, would it not be of interest to read what one bright-eyed little Indian girl wrote at the request of her teacher who asked her to write some story she had heard her father tell during long winter evenings. She insisted on spelling Indian in her own fashion. She was so interested in telling her story that she forgot about stopping for paragraphs so the author has given certain breathing spaces to the reader. Medicine Leaf is sixteen and was one of the girls chosen last spring to take tribal training in the home which she was not allowed to leave for some time. It is with her permission that I give her story. We talked about a few very obvious mistakes one evening in my home. Care has been taken to give it with very little editing. It is Medicine Leaf's story.

"TAOS INDIAN STORY"
By "Medicine Leaf"

Once upon a time there lived a rich Englishman[51] near the pueblo and the Taos Indains were living in

---

51. Medicine Leaf said she meant "white man." A man who speaks English is an Englishman to her.

TANOAN PEACE CEREMONY

Awa Tsireh

the Pueblo. One of a Indain woman was working
for this rich man. And one of a Indain boy was a
good friend to this rich man's son. And once the
Indains were going to hunt deers and the Indain boy
went to his friend to ask him to go and hunt. So they
went the last. And when they were already up the
mountains this boy of a rich man's wanted to drink
and he ask his friend if he knows where he could
drink and the Indain said to this boy Yes my friend
we are near the water but if you drink this water you
are going to turn to a deer. But the boy didn't
listen he just went straight to the water and drink.
So sure enough the boy had turn to a deer.

At last all the Indains that went to hunt go home
except that boy that turn to a deer so this rich man
asked the Indains where his son is but all the Indains
replyed that they don't know where he is. So this
rich man brought out the soldier and fought with the
Indains and have killed all the Indains except a lady
that was working for him. By and by this Indain
lady had a baby boy. And when this baby was getting big he ask his mother why they are dressed different than others. The lady said to her son My
dear we are Indains thats why we're dress different
than them.

Once there were a lot of Indains and the boys
and men went to hunt and this man's boy went to
hunt with the Indains and didn't return. So this
man brought the soldier and had killed all our Indains but he didn't kill me. That boy didn't return
because he turn to a great big deer. So this little
Indain boy asked again. Why did he return to a
deer. The mother replyed, ''My dear, he drank the

water where just the deers should drink and he turn
to a great deer with long white horns on. And the
boy said could I go and catch that deer? The mother
answered you may go my dear but do not kill him.
The little boy asked again do you know where the
water is and the lady said to her son. Yes my dear
come out with me and I will show you the way and
where it is so they both went outside and the mother
said to her son, do you see that big mountain up
there? She pointed up north. And the little boy said
yes. There is that water at the foot of this big mountain. So the little boy danced around and said to his
mother. ''Mother!'' hurry and make me bow and
arrows. So the mother went to work and got through
with and bow and arrow.

Just before the boy started the lady said to her
son. When you get there you will see a big tree with
a long branch sticking out. And you must sit on the
branch and watch the deers coming to drink the first
one that you will see is that boy. And when he come
near the water you must throw yourself down and
sit on his neck and fill[52] something on his neck with
your hand. When you fill something you take it out.
So the poor little boy started and when he got there
he did just what his mother had tellen him to do. So
when he took a stick out a deer skin fell off of the
boy. And the white boy was so glade to turn to a
human again. He thank that boy. And they start
off for home.

As they were on there way home the white boy
said to this Indain boy. When we get home take me

52. Feel.

to your house first and your mother will go to my father and tell him that you have brought me home. And when my father ask you what you want of his riches dont ask for any thing eles but his gold magic glass.[53] So by and by they got home and as they had planned to go to the Indain house first they went and when they went in the boy said Hello to this the lady and they were all very glade to see each others again. And they told this lady to go and tell the man that her son had brought his son home. So the lady went and told the rich man that his son had return home. And the man was so surprice and glade to know that his son had come home. He said to the Indain woman if you bring him to him I will give you all my riches. And the lady went back as fast she could so she and her son put that boy in the middle and took him to his father. As the man was so glade to see his son he said to the Indains now you may take what you want of my riches or eles take them all. But the Indain boy still remembered what the boy had said to him when they were coming home. So he said to this rich man. I want nothing eles besides your gold magic glass. "Alright," said the man so he gave a gold magic glass to the Indains. And the Indains happiely went back to their home. As soon as they got there a boy said to the glass, "Now my glass you are mine now so I want all the Indians that are dead to come alive again," so the glass did his power in the nite the next morning when they got up thier relations would come to see them. And all the Indain in the pueblo were alive again."

53. Perhaps Medicine Leaf had heard the story of Alladin's Lamp.

Probably when, in more serious mood, Medicine Leaf's father will tell of how the Chiffonettes came on earth. When the Indian forefathers were on their wanderings, they grew tired and faint from the hard way and the sun father pitied them and sent delight makers—the Koshares or Chiffonettes to make fun for them. They had corn leaves on their heads and they danced and sang for the people and made the corn to grow and the fruit to ripen. That is why there are fun-makers still in the pueblo.

But best of all is the story of the Indian's Messiah. "Montezuma" is the "Mexican name," they will tell you. They know him as Po-se-yemo. There are many stories about him but, in the Taos pueblo, old men tell how a great strange voice called across the meadows through the mist of a fall evening. Through fear none went out until finally names came to them through the twilight and then they all went out together. They found a wonderful man, taller than the willow bushes. He asked in a kindly voice why the corn did not grow on the meadows instead of weeds and wild flowers. They told him they did not know about corn. Then he taught them and stayed with them, ruling them the while. Finally came a sad day when the great One gave a feast and told the people that he must go away over the mountains alone. None must follow. Some day he would return. So he went away.[54]

For ages, the Indians have held a feast and played games on this day, now called San Geronimo.

---

54. These two stories were told to Charles F. Lummis, the noted writer of the Southwest.

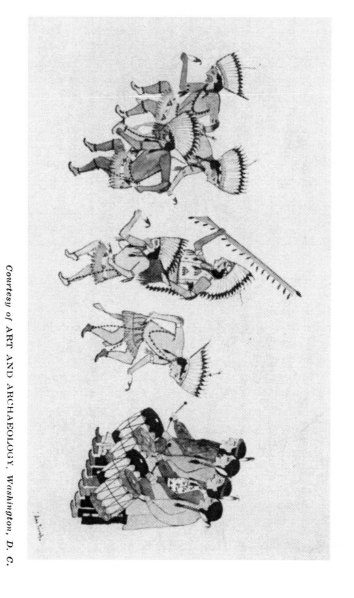

PUEBLO WAR DANCE

Awa Tsireh

They have watched for the return of Po-se-yemo night and day. Indeed it is said that is why they built the old wall around the pueblo so that there might be but two gates and here throughout the night many a young Indian has waited for the coming of the King so there would be some one to welcome him.

Now, there are no sentinels keeping an all-night vigil but the Taos Indians still believe that Po-se-yemo will come again. They live on quite happily together in their pueblos, "monuments to human love of home." There are only ripples on their stream of life—ripples that hint of the coming of the great whirlpool of the American nation. It will, however, still be a long time before the Taos Indians will be swept clear of their ancient moorings.

Sunny days still come and claim these farmer people. Twilight brings their songs. Midnight finds their high walls with tiny windows lost in the darkness of the kindly mountain standing ever by their side. Hearth fires scatter belated sparks through adobe chimneys. The whole pueblo sleeps—sleeps in very truth—while yonder on the old dark kiva altar glows the eternal fire—fire ready for the coming of Po-se-yemo.

THE TAOS EAGLE

PO-SE-YEMO

An unpublished manuscript by Ad. F. Bandelier, owned by Anthony Joseph of Ojo Caliente, N. M. Bandelier was one of the greatest scholars who ever came into the southwest. He worked here during the eighties.

The following piece of folk-lore concerning the Ruins and around Ojo Caliente has been gathered by me at San Juan de los Caballeros. My informants are the principal medicine-men of that pueblo, and the story was, subsequently, confirmed to me by the leading wizards of Santa Clara. There is no doubt therefore, that the tale, although incomplete, is still authentic, as far as its Indian origin is concerned, and that in so far it has no admixture of foreign elements.

The three pueblos of Homayo, Houiri, and Pose-uing-ge were built by the Tehuas, inhabited by them, and abandoned, centuries before the arrival of the Spaniards. At the time the last one named was still occupied, the Tehuas also dwelt in the caves above Santa Clara, at S. Juan and at Chamita. The pueblo at the latter place was called Yuge-uing-ge, the cave dwellings; Pu-ye and S. Juan bore its actual name of "Oj-ké." Pose-uing-ge was a flourishing village, its people had many green stones, many shell beads and similar Indian "treasures" for they controlled the boiling waters, and the latter were looked upon with awe by all the aborigines who came in contact with them. The spot was sacred to the "Trues."

Among the people of Pose-uinge-ge there was an

old woman who had an only daughter. One day that daughter went to the timber and, as she sat down under a Piñon-tree, a nut fell into her lap and then disappeared. Soon after, she discovered that she was pregnant, and when she brought forth a child in due time, that child was a boy. He was named Pose-yemo, afterward changed into Pose-ueve or "dew from heaven." Both his grandmother and mother were very poor, so that the child was always poorly clad, and as the other children of the pueblo jeered at him for his uncouth appearance, he became very shy and timid, and, as he grew up, was the laughing stock of the community for his ignorance, unkempt appearance, and clumsiness.

Pose-ueve was already a young man, when the Cacique of his village suddenly died. There was some difficulty about appointing a successor, as the deceased had not had time to communicate to anyone the dread secret that forms the nucleus of the duties and functions of the office. So, while the war-captain and his advisors, the leading principals, were still consulting on the matter, one of them suggested, in jest, that Pose-Ueve be selected. The joke was carried so far as to have the news of his election brought to the poor boy who became terribly frightened and went home in tears to tell his mother of the severe task about to be imposed upon him. To his astonishment, the mother encouraged him to accept the position and while they were talking, a stately eagle alighted on the roof of the house and gravely stalked into the room. The bird then spoke to the youth, telling him that it was of the "Trues" on

Courtesy of ART AND ARCHAEOLOGY, Washington, D. C.

PUSBLO INDIAN CEREMONIAL

Indian Artist

Courtesy of ART AND ARCHAEOLOGY, Washington, D. C.

BUFFALO PROCESSION

Awa Tsireh

high that he should become Cacique of Pose-uinge-ge, assuring him of their unfailing assistance, and giving him a great deal of important advice. Pose-Ueve became completely transformed. In place of the dirty and timid slouch, he presented himself before the principals as a handsome and neatly clad young man, who spoke well and earnestly, whose speech was wise as well as modest. His nomination as Cacique was at once confirmed, and with it began an era of prosperity unparalleled in the History of any new (word illegible) pueblo. Crops never failed. Yam was always abundant. The fame of Pose-Ueve spread to all the other tribes, for he was a powerful wizard, and the ''Trues'' never failed to respond to his calls for assistance.

One day he visited the pueblo of Yuge-uing-ge in disguise, but the people refused to recognize. This angered him in such a degree that he cursed them and disappeared forever. After his disappearance Pose-uinge-ge began to decline and was finally abandoned, the remainder of its people moving south, there to join the other Tehuas. The causes of this abandonment of Ojo Caliente are variously stated, stories of magic and witchcraft playing the principal part. Houiri and Homayo had been previously abandoned.

Pose-Ueve is known to the Quires as ''Pshaya,'' to the Zunis as ''Pusha-iankio.'' These tribes believed (him) to have been a mighty wizard, attributing to him the institution of many dances, rites, and even of most of their religious organizations. The name Montezuma is an importation from Mex-

ico, and has nothing to do with the genuine pueblo
folk-tale above related.

It seems certain that Pose-Ueve was an histori-
cal personage, some "medicine-man" of great fame,
who lived at Ojo Caliente several centuries previous
to the sixteenth and whose fame as well as influence
spread over a considerable portion of New Mexico.
Such personages, afterwards diefied, occur frequently in tradition and folklore of the Indians.

Signed
Ad. F. Bandelier

Bandelier drew a small map of the Ojo Caliente
country, showing Po-se Uing-ge (dew drop) as the
pueblo nearest to the present town of Ojo Caliente,
the pueblo of Hom-a-yo (the fawn) as almost due
north of Pose-Uing-ge on the same side of the river
while he puts Ho-uir-i as across the river and somewhat to the northeast of Homayo. Houiri he says
meant "Butterfly." His spelling of the various
pueblos is not always the same. Bandelier adds a
note, "Po-se Yemo monarch and medicine man in
1450 & resided at Po-se Uing-ge."

The story as here given copied from the original
manuscript does appear in various forms in some of
Bandelier's writings but the owner says he believes
this particular version has never been published and

55. Ojo Caliente or Hot Springs is a little town about thirty-five
or forty miles west of Taos. It takes its name naturally from
the famous hot springs at the foot of the hills across the little
river. So remarkable are the cures which take place at the
springs, if those who suffer are willing to remain long enough for
the arsenic water to take effect, that one is tempted to say nothing but urge those who are doubtful to come and see for themselves. It is indeed no wonder that the early Spaniards who tar-
ried at these "boiling waters" of the Indians believed they had
discovered a veritable fountain of youth.

that it was written at the request of Mr. Joseph's father for his two children. The manuscript has been in the possession of the Joseph family for many years. The writer is indebted to Anthony Joseph for permission to publish this story.

BOOKS ABOUT TAOS

Taos—One Hundred Years Ago $ .75

Taos Today 1.00

Taos Indians 1.00

Postage 10 cents each.

by

Blanche C. Grant
Taos, New Mexico

Drawn by Kenneth M. Chapman. The design is taken from San Ildefonso pottery and signifies, in general, water. Clouds, the curves below, bring rain and leaf forms spring up. The outer design of curves with the point means rain for other people.

Index

Printed in the United States
207347BV00001B/350/A